Luciano Fabro

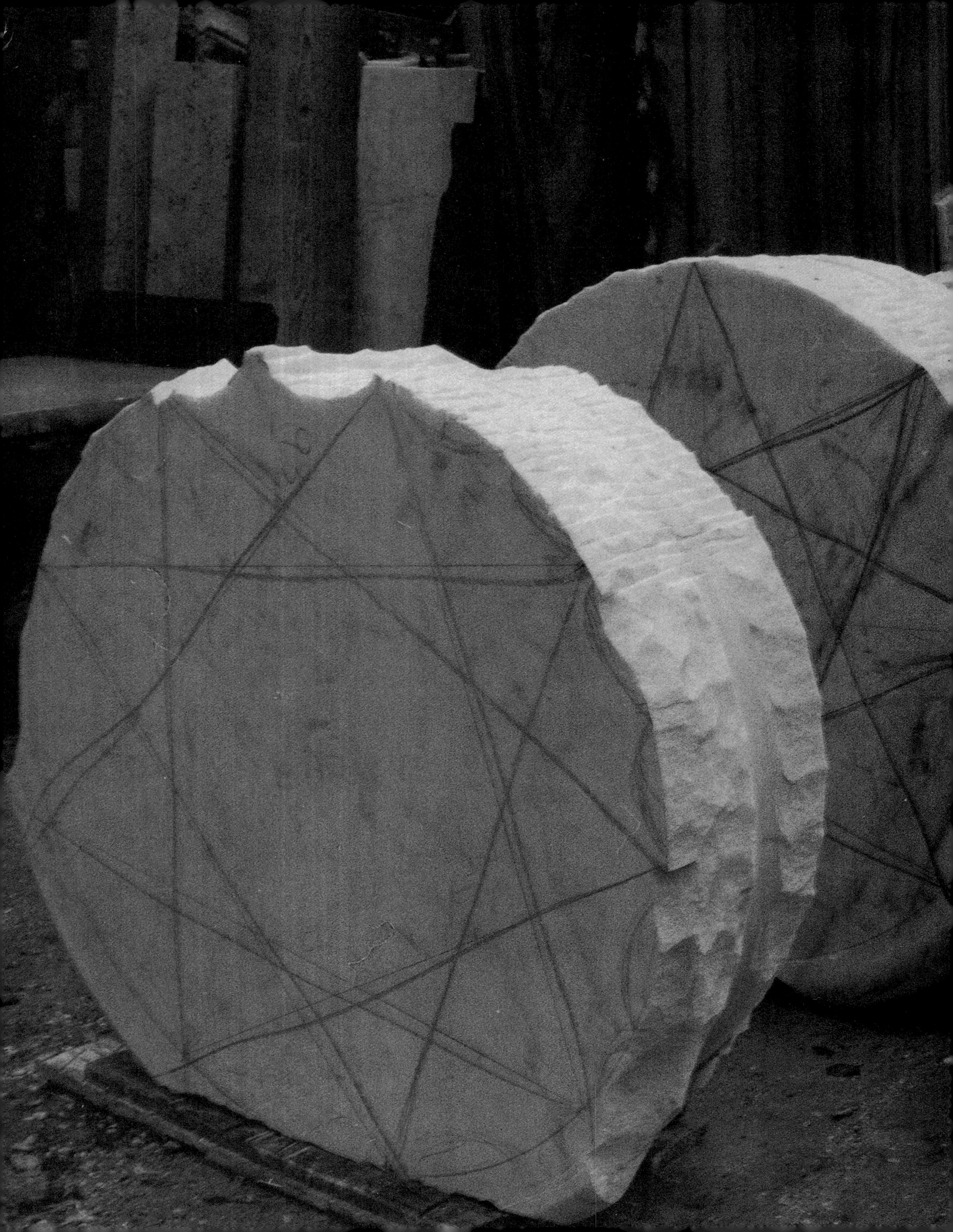

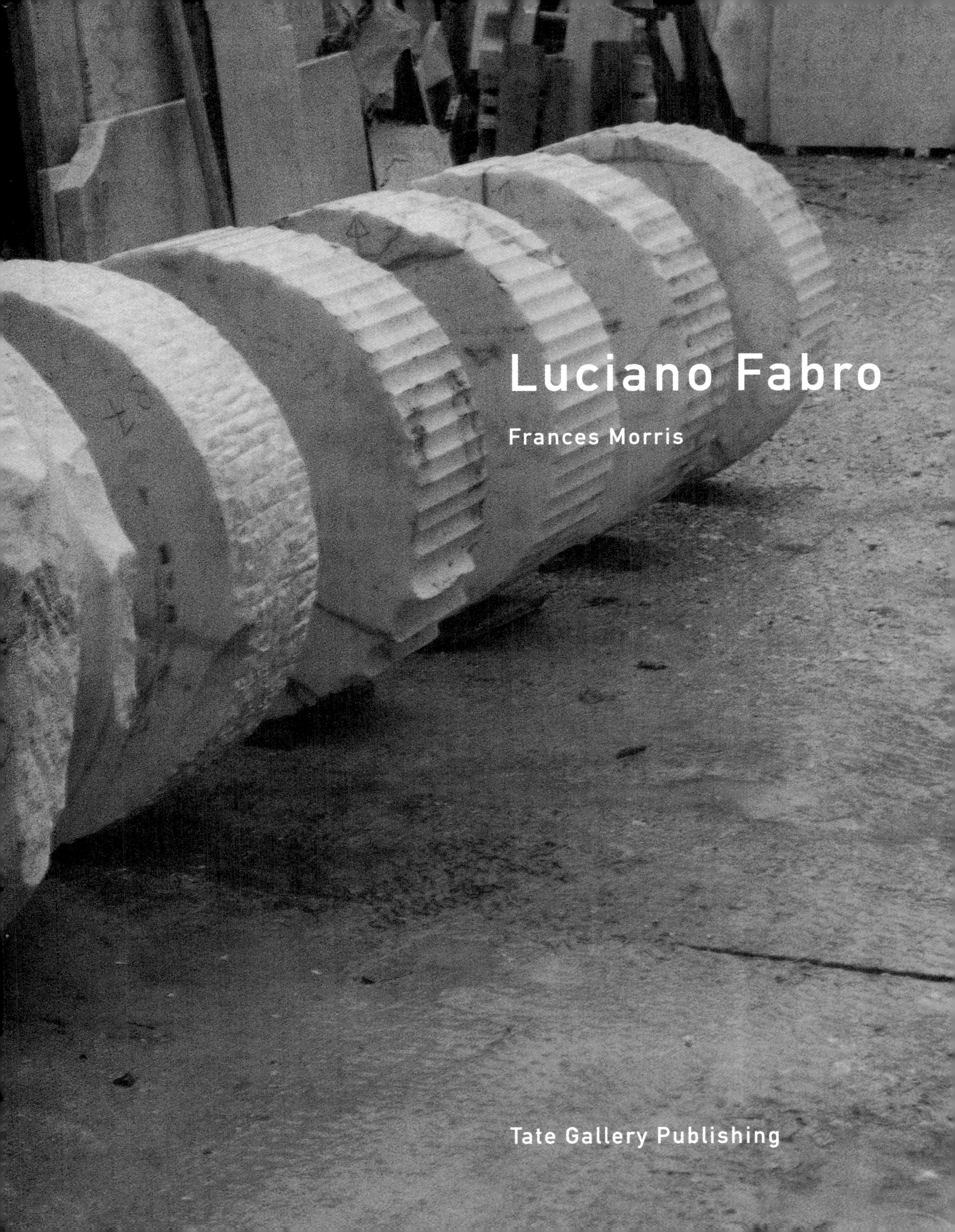

Luciano Fabro

Frances Morris

Tate Gallery Publishing

Published by order of the Trustees
of the Tate Gallery 1997
by Tate Gallery Publishing Ltd
Millbank, London SW1P 4RG

ISBN 0 85437 235 1

This catalogue is published to accompany
the exhibition at the Tate Gallery
11 February – 15 June 1997

Supported by the Coutts Contemporary
Art Foundation and the Friends of the Tate Gallery

A catalogue record for this book is available
from the British Library

Designed and typeset by Martin Brown
Printed in Great Britain by M & TJ Print Ltd

Frontispiece Luciano Fabro, *Il Sole (The Sun)*,
work in progress, Carrara 1996

Contents

Foreword

Over the last thirty years Luciano Fabro has maintained a high international profile as an artist of singular interest and fierce independence. Fabro has always eschewed a signature style and employs a wide range of materials and techniques in works that are always surprising, arresting and challenging. His art appears to achieve a balance between the sensual and the intellectual and rewards time and effort on the part of the viewer.

This exhibition is the result of a happy coincidence between our desire to invite the artist to exhibit his work at the Tate Gallery and his own long expressed interest in the architecture of the Sackler Octagon and the Duveen Galleries. We are delighted that this interest has resulted in the making of *Il Sole* and *La Luna*, two sculptures in marble which Fabro has made in response to these spaces and which explore the complex meanings bound up in the symbolism of architectural structures. These works are documented in the catalogue which contains an essay by Frances Morris, Assistant Keeper in the Modern Collection who has worked closely with the artist throughout the preparation of the exhibition.

In 1994 Fabro was awarded the Coutts Contemporary Art Award and the Coutts Contemporary Art Foundation has generously supported this exhibition. We offer our sincere thanks to them and to the Friends of the Tate Gallery who have also made funds available.

We are enormously grateful to Fabro himself for his assistance at every stage. Not only has he been involved in the preparation of the catalogue and in the design for the cover and for the poster but he has also dedicated a considerable amount of time to the exhibition itself. It has been a real pleasure to work with him.

Nicholas Serota
Director

Luciano Fabro:
In Virtue of References

One evening in 1989, after dinner at a restaurant in Milan, I was taken by Luciano Fabro to his studio. The artist had been a curious and entertaining dinner companion. A short drive from the restaurant brought us to a quiet street lined with the kind of anonymous and self-effacing façades that are typical of Milan. Fabro's studio was reached through a main entrance on the street and across a small inner courtyard surrounded by high white walls. Access to the inner sanctum of an artist one admires can give a privileged view of their working methods, in close proximity to tools and models: it can be an occasion for revelations and understanding. On this evening I was disappointed as we entered a pair of small rooms distinguished, at first sight, by an invasive harsh light and a sense of vacancy.

In one corner, however, lay a slab of lusciously veined, pale grey marble. The contours of finely carved drapery revealed the form of a male figure resembling a recumbent tomb effigy. The figure had no head: at the junction of drapery and pillow the human form subsided, leaving nothing of substance beyond the body other than the imprint of a head on the marble pillow. Not content with leaving the impression of this strange act of disappearance to take root in the viewer's imagination, Fabro had inscribed the work on opposite sides of the base: 'Dal pieno al vuolto senza soluzione di continuità' and 'Io rappresento l'imgonbro dell'oggetto nella vanità dell'ideologia' ('From the Full to the Empty without any solution of continuity' and 'I represent the obstruction of the object in the vanity of ideology'). These lines seem to warn us against a direct transaction between image and idea, they create a block in the flow of references to sources, both living and dead, whether from classical art history, contemporary news pictures or from biblical scenes of death and resurrection. They call us to pause on the verge of iconographic analysis, for there is an obstruction, there is no solution. The obstruction is the material, obdurate and imposing; matter through which the artist has drawn attention to the opposite, non-matter, and thus, by implication, presence and absence. So the work entitled *Lo Spirato (The Deceased)* is not so much an image of death as an image of the transformation of the body into something else: of body into spirit, of matter into void and of past into present.

With its richly sensuous material, its pointed iconographical references and its enigmatic, probing inscriptions, *Lo Spirato* seems at odds with Fabro's spare, abstract experiments of the years prior to its making. It was made over a five year period, from 1968 to 1973, first in plaster and then in marble. Fabro first exhibited his work in 1965, with a show at the Galleria Vismara in Milan. The exhibition included a number of pieces made in glass or metal which explored the functioning of materials and forms in real space and the identity of the work within the physical and perceptual environment created by the viewer. *Buco (Hole)* of 1963 (fig.2) and *Tondo e rettangolo (Circle and Rectangle)* of 1964 (fig.4) used the transparent and reflective characteristics of glass to explore space and the perception of space – the artwork was both a window on the world, and a reflection or imitation of it. In *Buco* a sheet of glass is spattered with areas of opaque and reflective material. Unable to see through the glass without simultaneously seeing what is reflected, the viewer experiences the coexistence of direct sensation and mediated experience. More minimal in appearance is Fabro's 1964 *Ruota (Wheel)* (fig.3), made from stainless steel, in which a circle of metal is welded onto a steel pole hinged from the wall. The length of the pole corresponds to the circumference of the circle. Simple to describe or draw on a sheet of paper, the work functions only in real time and space, establishing its own uneasy equilibrium as the weight of the circle causes the arm to curve away from the perpendicular. At the same time an apparent sensation of motion is created as the circle appears to roll down the line.

At around the time of the Galleria Vismara exhibition Fabro first met Germano Celant, originator of the term 'Arte Povera' and

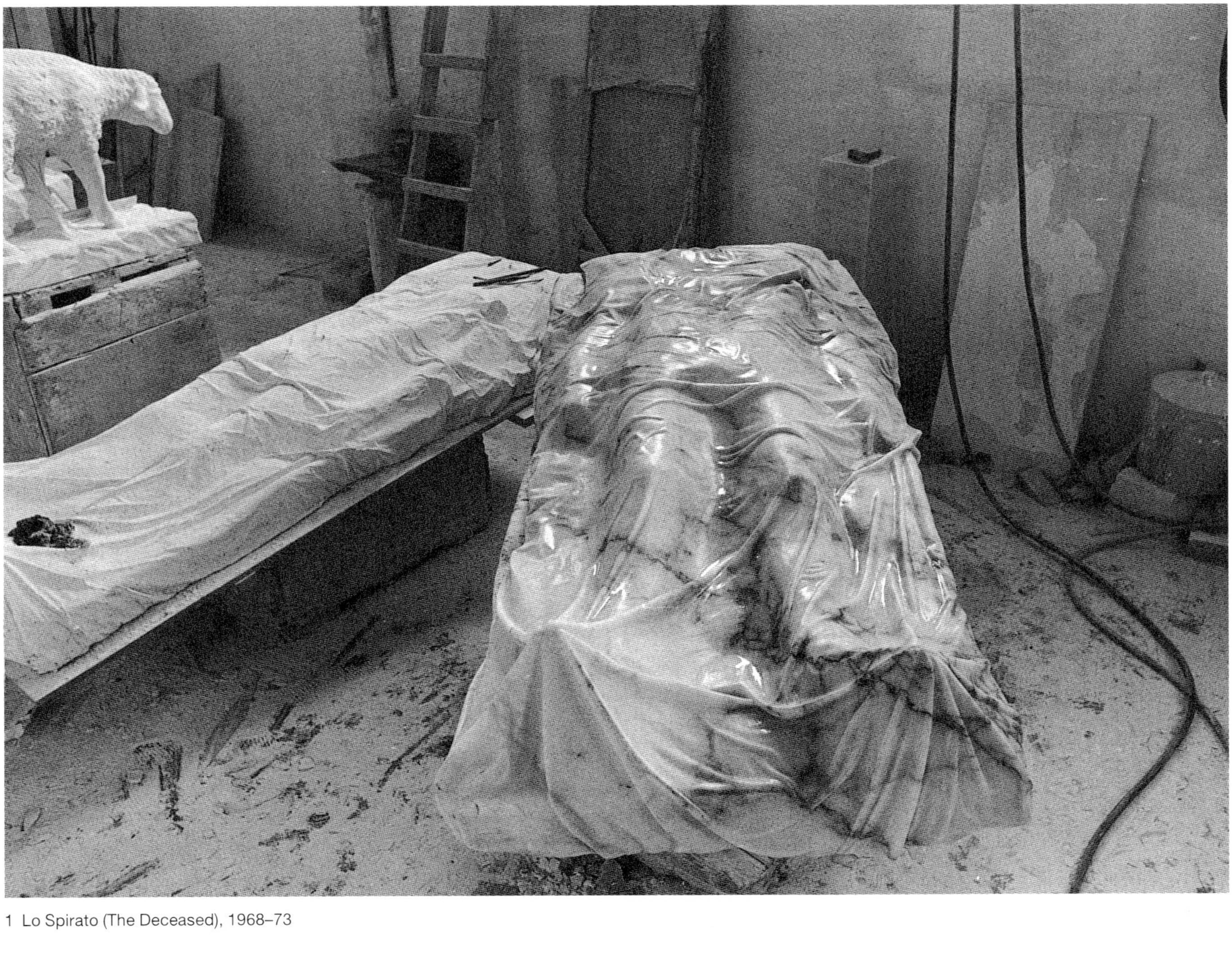
1 Lo Spirato (The Deceased), 1968–73

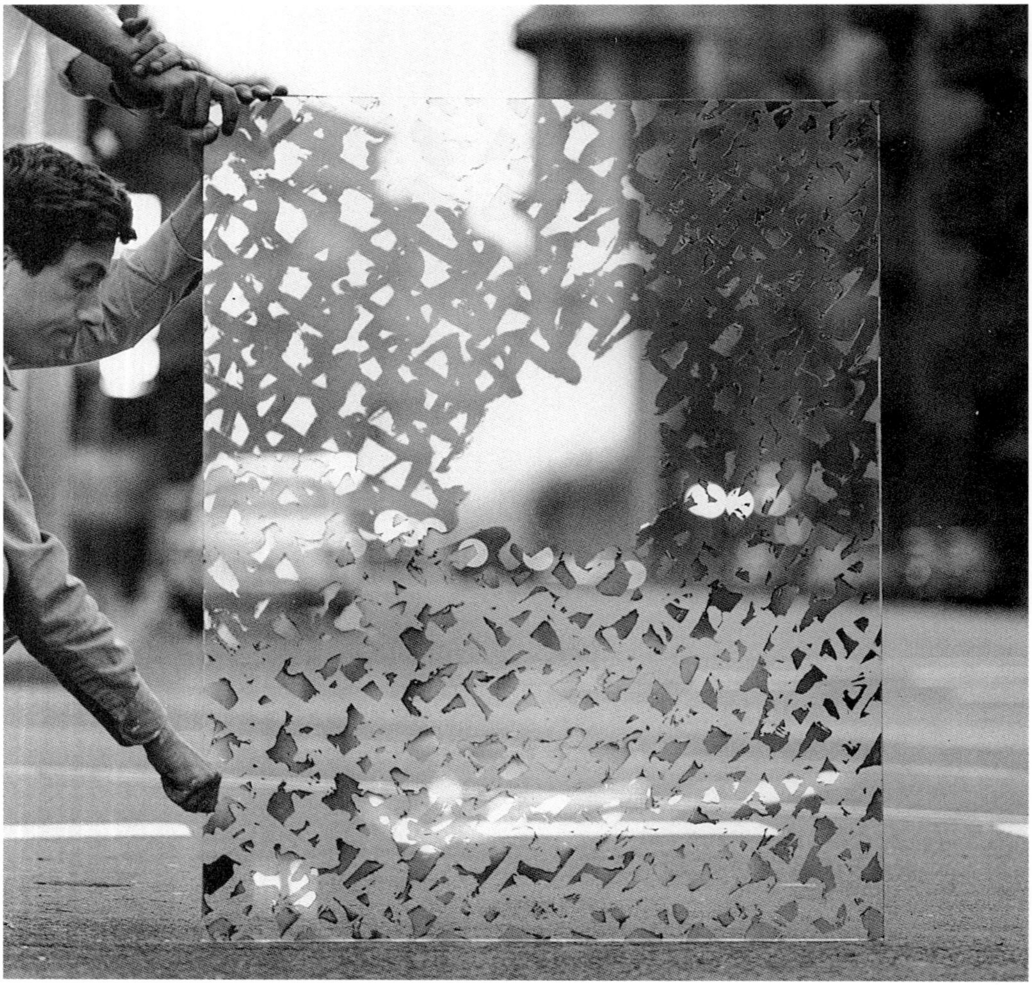

2 Buco (Hole), 1963

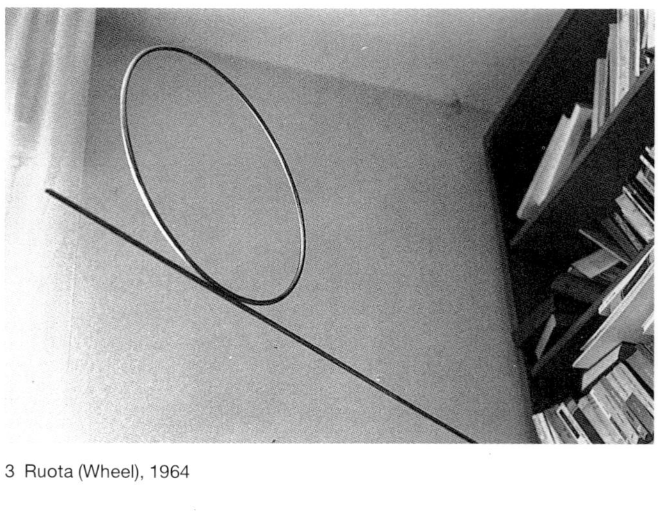

3 Ruota (Wheel), 1964

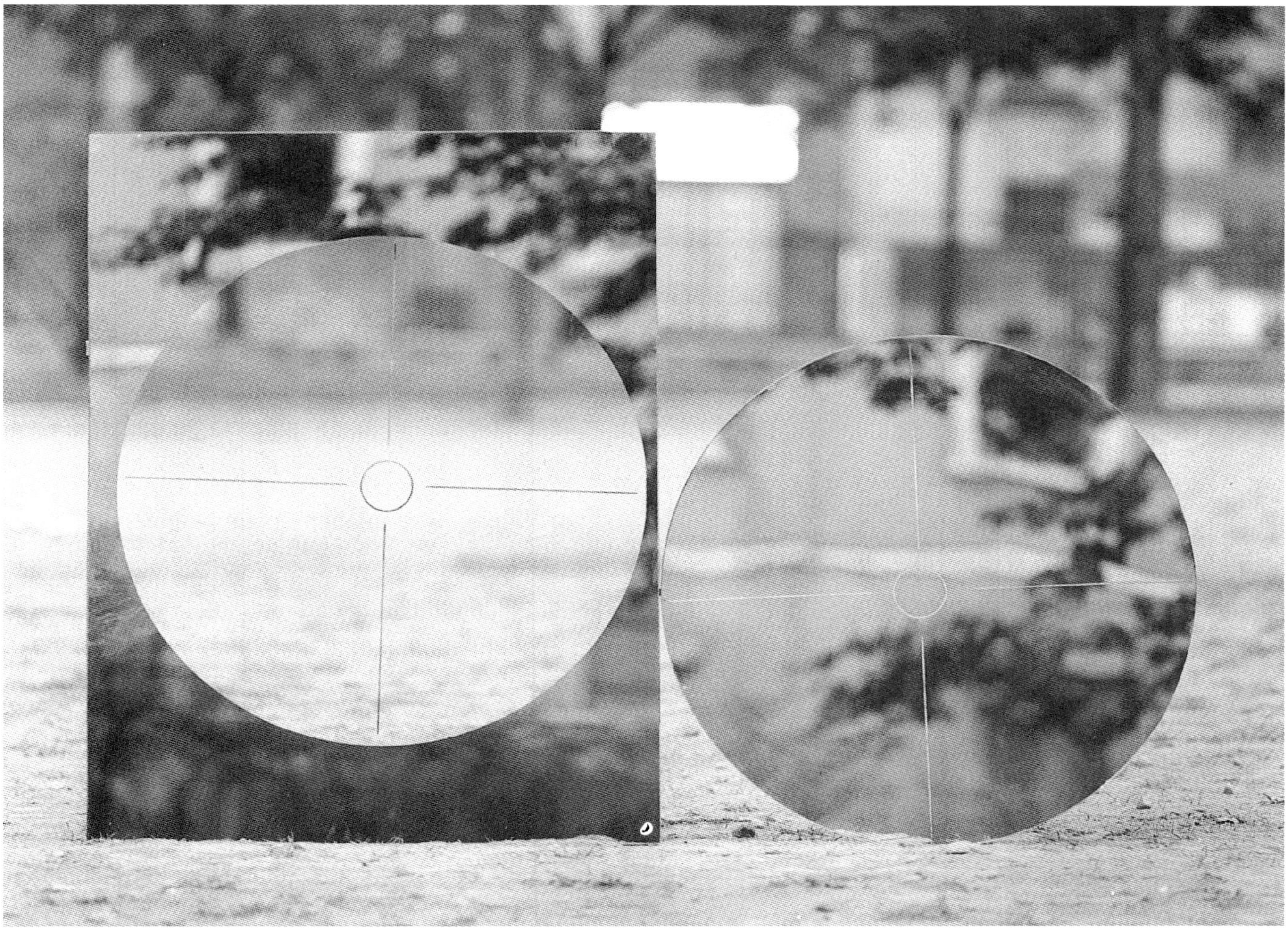
4 Tondo e rettangolo (Circle and Rectangle), 1964

prime mover behind the series of exhibitions that brought the artist into close dialogue with a group of his contemporaries which included Mario Merz, Jannis Kounellis and Michelangelo Pistoletto. These artists, working against the grain of minimalism, sought to widen the base for art by employing materials not previously associated with fine art and by exploring new ways of making art, including performance and work made outside the gallery or studio. While Arte Povera swiftly became international in scope it emerged out of specifically Italian aesthetic experiments pioneered by Lucio Fontana, Alberto Burri and Piero Manzoni, who created the ground for Arte Povera's further explorations of real space (as opposed to the fictional space of painting), commonplace materials and the gesture of the artist.

In the catalogue of his Galleria Vismara show Fabro described his interest in the physical qualities of materials: 'In all cases, the use of material has been determined by human experience of which it is an especially able reporter (elasticity, luminosity, transparency, reflection, refraction ...). My practical problem is not then that of rendering an otherwise amorphous material aesthetic, but rather that of rendering as clearly as possible the natural dialogue with the material'.[1] Elsewhere Fabro warned against reading his work in terms of preconceived interpretation for 'rather than one particular type of interpretation, I would like to show the viewer how to read the experience, the things themselves'.[2] As for space, Fabro was acutely aware of its dual nature as object and metaphor, for space is the result of a sensorial experience: 'Just as a bent piece of iron expresses the force that was exerted upon it, just like a thrown stone gives a centre to the borders of a puddle, a finger indicates the direction of a gaze; in the same manner, we move in a space by means of solicitations of impressions'.[3]

Fabro was keenly interested in the way in which we experience and interpret situations and images, and was aware of both the expansive and reductive potential of aesthetic procedures. In the group of works which is subtitled *Tautologies* (1967 and 1968), references (to domestic situations, experiences of nature, familiar symbols) were decontextualised or internalised in order to create a kind of implosion of meaning. *Foro Ø 8mm – Tautologia (8mm Ø Perforation – Tautology)*, 1967, comprised a sheet of industrially perforated stainless steel. The artist had made a new perforation, identical to the others, in the centre. In the same year *Pavimento – Tautologia (Floor – Tautology)* was made from a series of domestic tiles. The work was covered with newspapers but required frequent cleaning and covering over again. As Fabro said at the time, 'Constant maintenance is necessary so that the postulated conditions are kept. What's more, all experience of this article is limited to its maintenance'.[4]

Fabro described these works made in 1967 and 1968 as 'a kind of immunisation cure'. In a text entitled *Settembre 1967* he characterised his situation as one of 'attentive waiting', and mapped out his aim of moving on from the *tabula rasa* exposed by these exercises 'in order to be able to work with what is full and well-resolved in its attributes – with precisely the virtuoso hope of leaving attributes behind'.[5] This planned 're-routing' led to a new attitude to materials and the introduction of culturally contingent iconography: *Lo Spirato* was started in 1968.

The first sculpture in the *Italia* series (figs.7–9) was also made in 1968 and was followed by dozens more over the coming years. 'Italy is an image for anybody who feels in some way bound to it, whose shape is seen as a graphic of ideas', said the artist.[6] In these works Fabro adopted the geographical outline of Italy as his template, and has transformed it through his use of materials so that the template becomes a tool capable of many uses, a 'thinking model' generating very different images, each caught in a web of associations: hung upside down, his Italy appears to reverse the politico-economic north-south divide in the nation

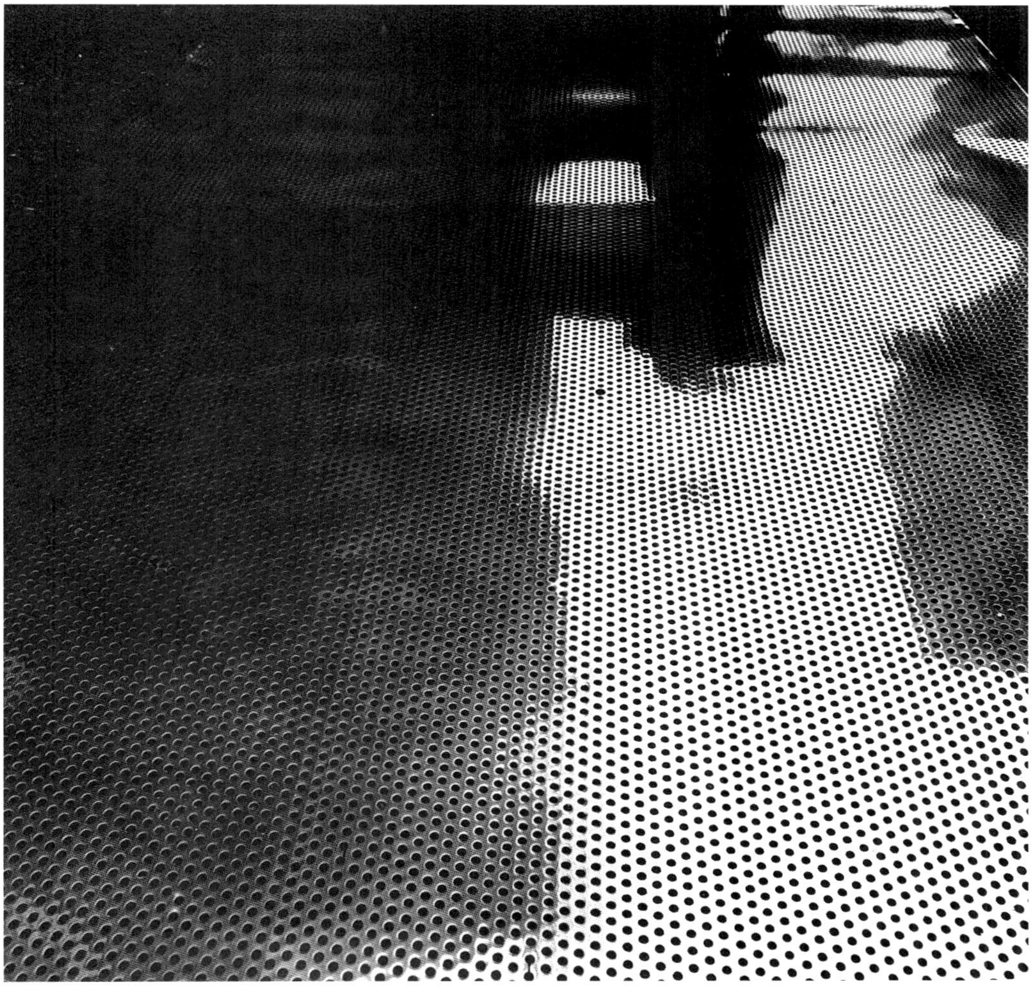

5 Foro Ø 8mm – Tautologia (8mm Ø Perforation – Tautology), 1967

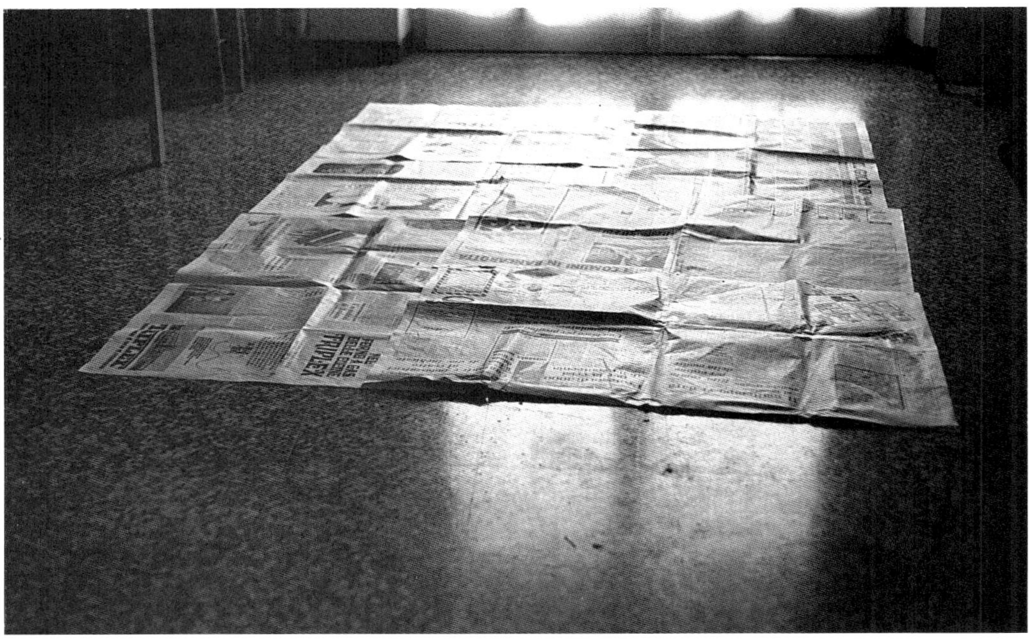

6 Pavimento – Tautologia (Floor – Tautology), 1967

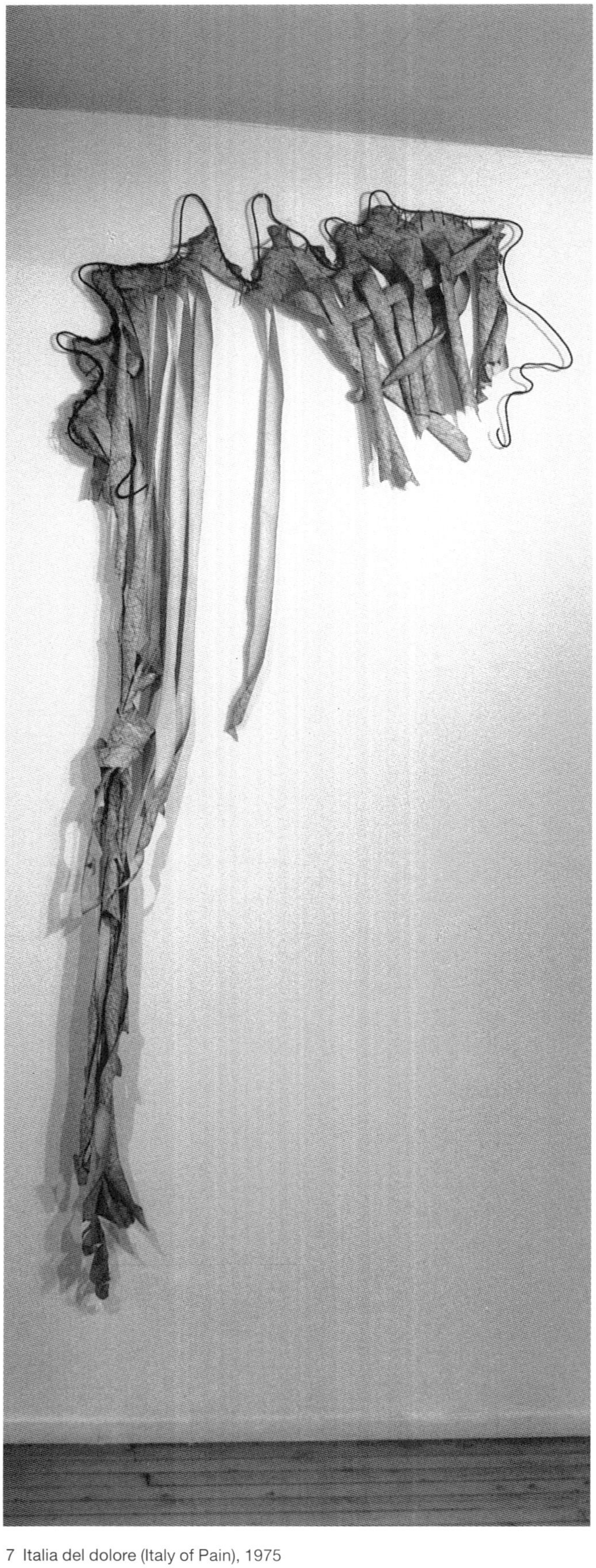

7 Italia del dolore (Italy of Pain), 1975

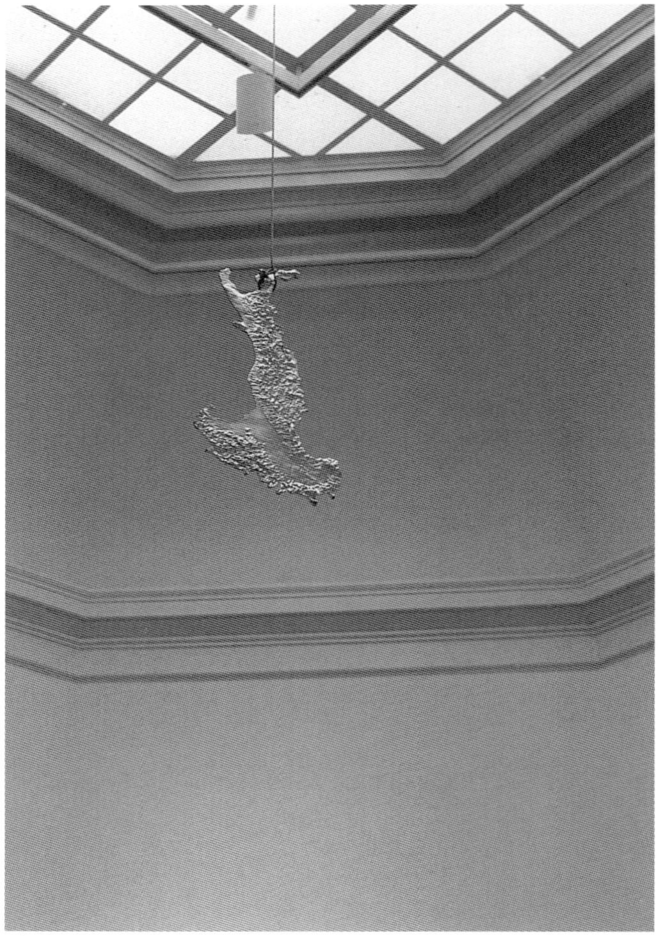

8 Italia d'oro (Golden Italy), 1971

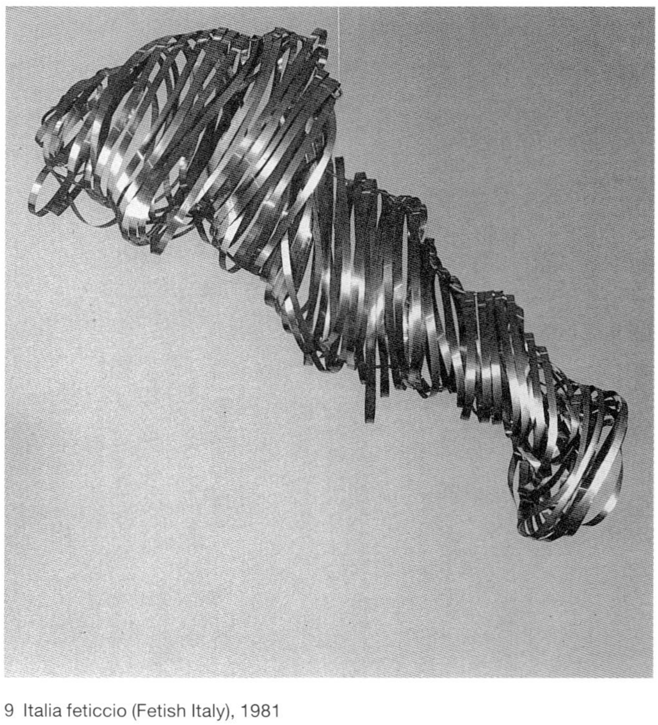

9 Italia feticcio (Fetish Italy), 1981

and also enhances the peninsula's physical resemblance to a dismembered body. In *Italia d'oro (Golden Italy)* of 1971 the form and terrain of the country in all its richly furrowed contours is impressed in gilded bronze. *Italia del dolore (Italy of Pain),* 1975, is a road map attached to a canvas in the shape of Italy, and hung in wide strips from an iron bar. *Italia feticcio (Fetish Italy),* 1981, was made from a loose core of metal tubing hung from the centre of an eighteenth-century dome, the template used here, largely for formal reasons, as a means of exploring the closed spiral. Collectively the *Italia* works draw attention to the rootedness of our lives, to the land we inhabit. All our experiences and those of people in history, our culture, our architecture, arise from an encounter between ourselves and the land. The meanings we ascribe to things, from the great physical discoveries over the centuries to the most transient human gesture, return at base to the geological mass we stand on.

Piedi (Feet) (fig.10) was another typographical model first explored in 1968 and presented as a group in 1971. Each *Piede* comprised a base element resembling the foot or claw of a more or less convincing animal species with a tall willowy leg or stocking in fabric. The feet themselves were made in various materials – in polished metal, and later in glass, but mostly in types of marble finished to differing degrees – so that while one foot seems to be held on a brink of figuration, others appear convincingly real. The stocking legs were made in silk, skillfully pressed, and detailed with often elaborate pleatings and gatherings. These are extraordinary and bizarre works – high fashion meeting the Natural History Museum – in which the conjunction between materials and imagery seems unfathomable in rational terms. Two things at least are clear: that Fabro, with awareness, was working within a framework of cultural associations, in the 'shadow of ancient sculpture' (from piede comes 'piedistallo' or pedestal), and that his desire was to bring to the fore the overt physicality of the work: 'it is plasticity that determines the revelation that is called sculpture … Revelation is like being introduced into the mystery of the image through the materials: the innate strength of all things physical that is found in their material forms'.[7]

Over his career Fabro has employed a bewildering variety of materials. Art, for him, is simultaneously a physical experience and a perceptual activity, in both its inception and its reception; materials are the physical interface between the artist and viewer. Generally, but not exclusively, Fabro employs materials in their natural state and transforms them through craft and in combination with other materials. The materials themselves are references. The textiles he uses frequently denote, for Fabro, the humble labours of anonymous women. Cloth ages faster than many other materials but its presence draws attention to the inevitable ageing of all natural materials. Fabro's recurrent use of marble should be seen in the context of his Italian backgound – in Carrara the pavements are laid in marble. It serves him in many ways. In *La nascita di Venere (The Birth of Venus)* of 1992 (fig.11), marble acts as, among other things, a conduit of tradition. In contrast marble can be a relatively neutral carrier of form. Fabro used marble to develop a curved slab logotype through which to represent the naked female body – as seen, for example, in *Due nudi che scendono le scale ballando il Boogie-Woogie (Two Nudes Descending a Staircase Dancing the Boogie-Woogie)* of 1989 (fig.13). Elsewhere, in *Kronus*, 1991 (fig.12), the material, rough hewn, declares itself an ancient geological substance. A complex play of differing sensations is unleashed by Fabro in *Il giorno mi pesa sulla notte (Day Weighs On Me At Night)* of 1995 (see colour plates), in which two types of marble, variously tooled, are placed amidst a scattering of children's glass marbles.

Often a work will emerge from thinking about or encountering a physical situation. *Il Giudizio di Paride (The Judgement of Paris)* of 1979 (fig.15) arose from Fabro's experience of the tactile quality of the material (clay) and the way in which he could create a

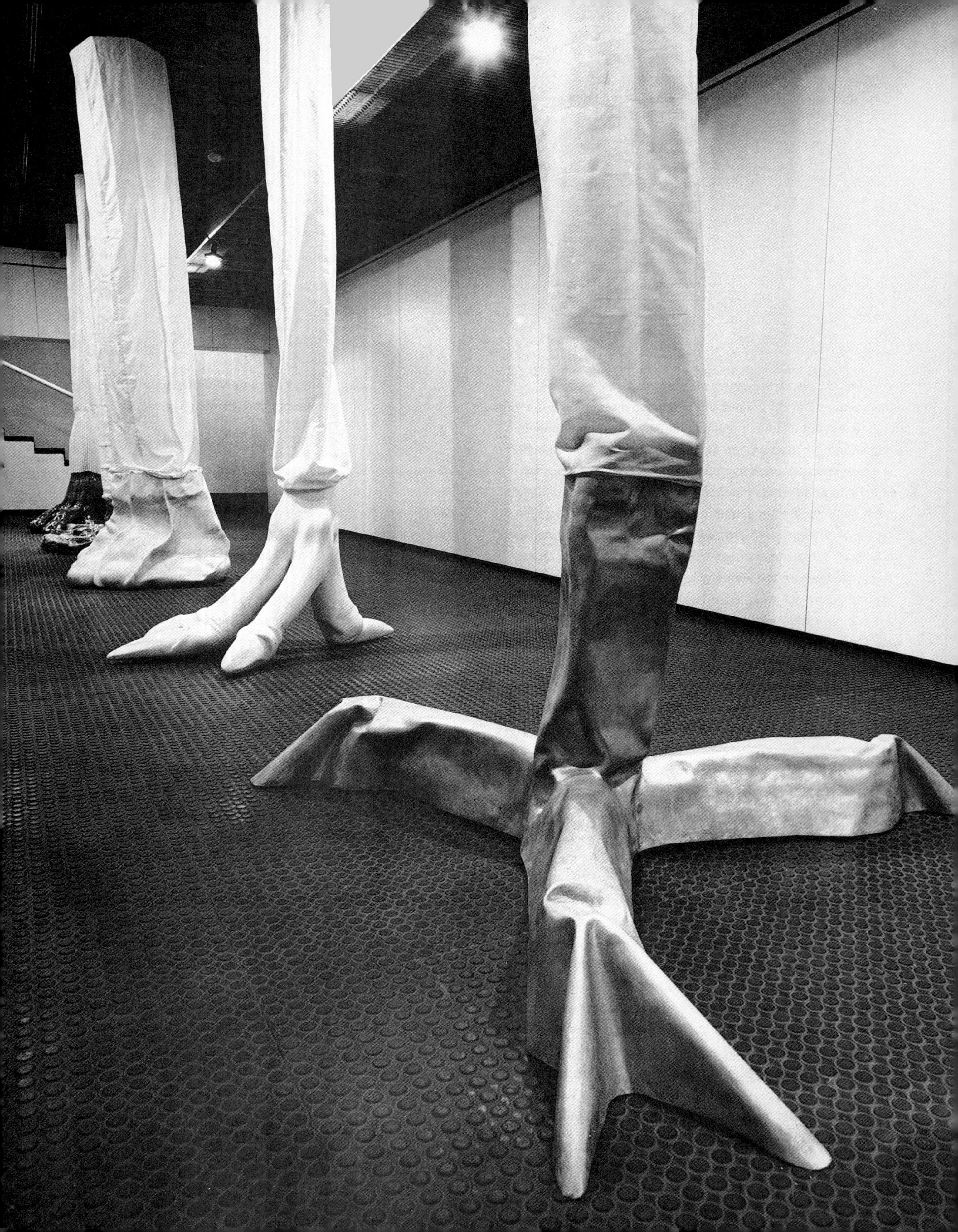

10 Piedi (Feet), 1968–71

different surface for each form using his hands. Other works arise in meditation on art and nature. Fabro made *Esprit de géométrie, esprit de finesse (Spirit of Geometry, Spirit of Finesse)* in 1984 (fig.24): a column of Zebrino marble fluted according to two alternative 'systems', one in which the natural veins of the marble determine the fluting, the other in which the classical model of regularly disposed grooves is followed. Crucial to his way of working is the charge of energy created when putting one material in relation to another. Fabro himself instanced this in a recent discussion of *Ovaie (Ovaries)* of 1988 (fig.14). He described the charge effected by the marriage of marble eggs and steel cable as 'sympathy', for the two very different elements meet in a relationship which both guarantees their individual identities and at the same time produces a new expressive dimension. Elsewhere Fabro has stated: 'when, let us say, I join bronze and copper, one colour to another colour, I create a metaphysical form of sympathy, and thus when the result of the union functions, we no longer have the sense of the union, but a sense of a third thing'.[8]

Fabro's description of the genesis of the *Piedi* demonstrates his empirical approach to sculpture-making: 'There are certain works that are born simply from a series of favourable circumstances among which it would be hard to establish any order of precedence: a critical moment in the general situation, the personal impulse of the artist, the availability of means such as money, or of instruments such as the technical capacity to produce the work or have it produced, or else the special resonance that the artist feels around him at the time'.[9] Elsewhere, even more starkly, Fabro speaks of the way an image arrives, as it were, fully formed in his imagination. This is not to say that Fabro's images come from nowhere. On the contrary, the field is limitless. He draws on experiences and observations in daily life, experiences of the imagination, ideas fuelled by his extensive reading, his reflection on art history, philosophy, science and politics. This range is accompanied by a firmly held

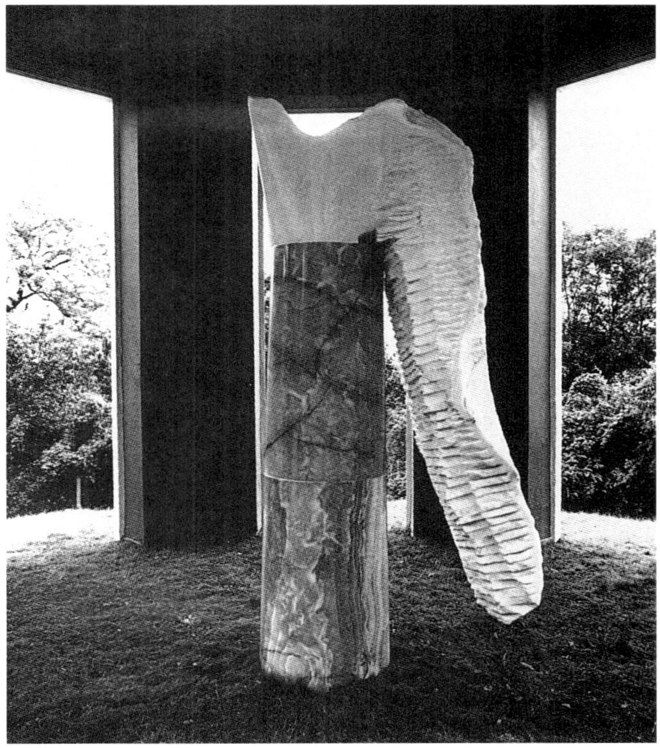

11 La nascita di Venere (The Birth of Venus), 1992

belief that all matters of import, today as well as in the past, are continually open to question and need to be readdressed if only to guarantee our cultural tradition. The manner in which his reflections represent themselves as art is sometimes complex, sometimes extremely direct, but almost always develops through an essentially intuitive process. This accounts for the apparent unpredictability of his art, an unpredictability that extends, as we have already seen, to the materials he uses and the crafts that he employs. It also explains the apparent absence of stylistic coherence, of a formal trajectory through his career, and his practice of representing earlier work in new contexts without any sense of curatorial retrospection.

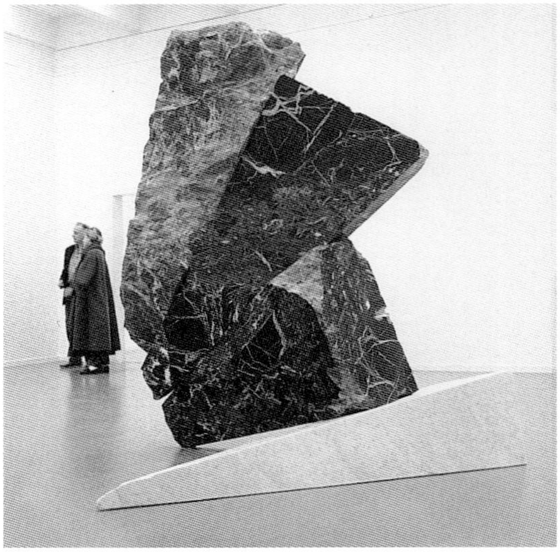

12 Kronus, 1991

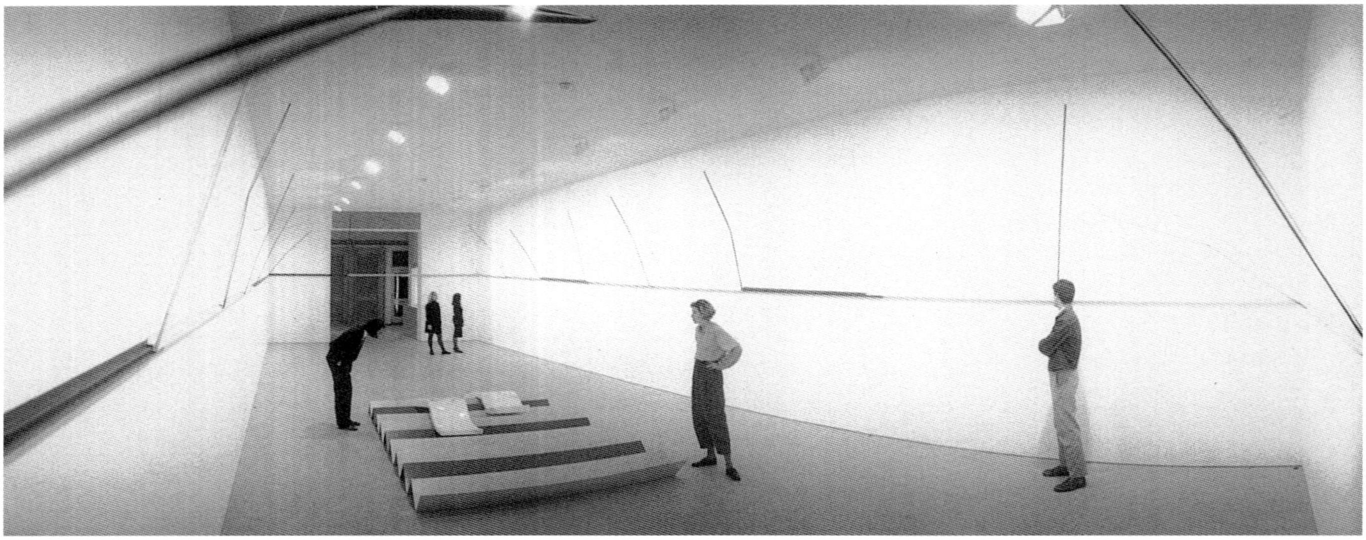

13 Due nudi che scendono le scale ballando il Boogie-Woogie (Two Nudes Descending a Staircase Dancing the Boogie-Woogie), 1989

14 Ovaie (Ovaries), 1988

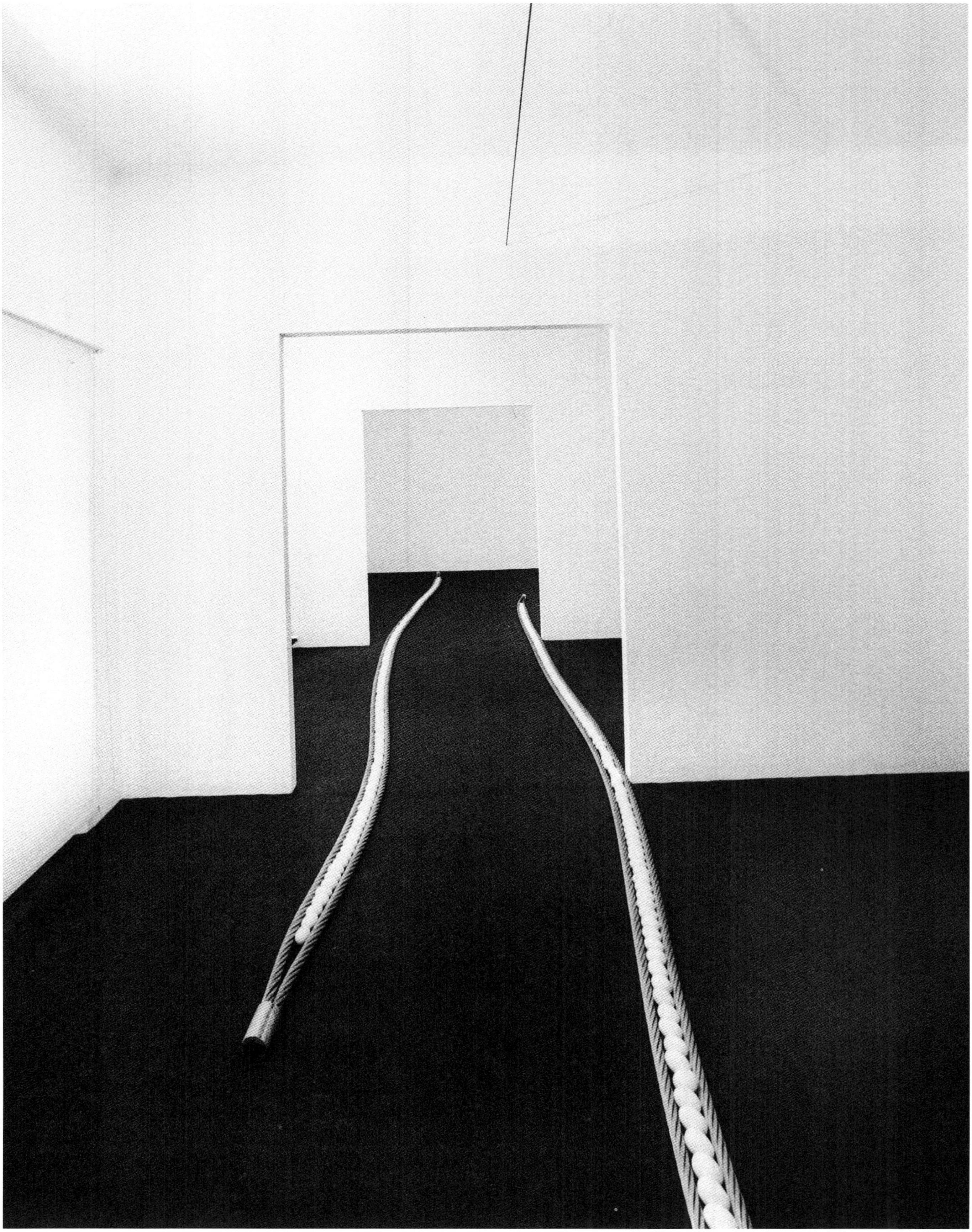

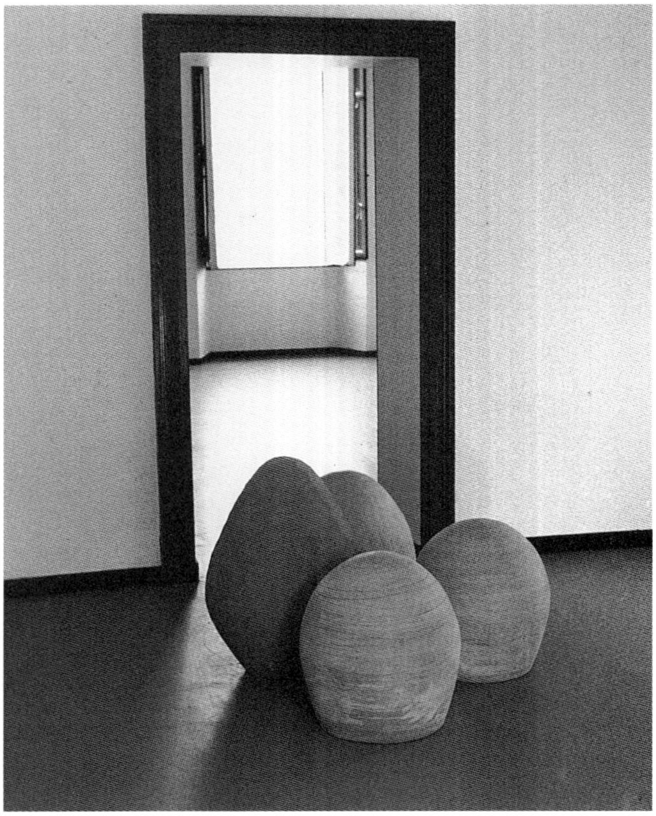

15 Il Giudizio di Paride (The Judgement of Paris), 1979

Fabro's own metaphor for his life's course and his aesthetic stance is taken from Lawrence Sterne. Sterne's novel *The Life and Opinions of Tristram Shandy*, pubished in 1759, is commonly regarded as the precedent for the stream-of-consciousness novel of the twentieth century. The story is narrated by Tristram – 'Shandy', a term whose origins are obscure, means 'half-crazy' – in a disordered sequence of events, interrupted by extended digressions and avoiding any plot or conclusion. Even the typology of the text is erratic, with rows of asterisks, dashes, varied typefaces and other devices used to depart from the norm. In chapter 40, volume 6 of the novel, graphic zigzag motifs are employed to symbolise the author's meandering narrative line. According to Fabro, 'The schematic zigzags which interrupt the body of the text introduce an image of real experience, not a formal literary structure. When Sterne skipped two chapters (which he then inserted five chapters later), it was his way of stating that the reader had total freedom to go on with the story. The blank pages were a way of saying "On the strength of your experience, you go on from here"'.[10]

Fabro borrowed Sterne's motif to illustrate his 1978 book of writings *Attaccapanni (Clothes-hangers)* which bound together texts from the past in 'a continuous narrative flux with interior memories and notes on writing'.[11] Fabro's texts demonstrate an intellectual mobility that at its lightest moments casts the author as dandy and at its most profound reveals a Renaissance spirit of enquiry and erudition.

'The nature of my fantasy, my senses, my intelligence, my culture, provides me with images; I attempt to relay these images to others through my work.'[12] Since making the *Piedi*, Fabro has repeatedly demonstrated that his fantasy, senses and intelligence operate on the widest cultural terrain, mining seams in art and literature, mythology, history and the sciences as if all aspects of human understanding were continuously open to interrogation and reflection. He is interested in those concepts and characters in history, real and fictional, which have been dedicated to understanding and making sense of the world, and practices like geometry and astrology which shaped mankind's spiritual and social patterns for generations. The scope and implications of such enquiries have been long since diminished by their progressive division into specialist compartments. Fabro sees the interconnectedness of these realms, and their coexistence in past and present, as the province of art.

At a time when so much contemporary art practice is conceptually based and uses the tools of representation such as symbol and metaphor to identify ideas, how are we to read Fabro's works with their complex layering and interconnections of meaning? One way might be to take the example of mythology, and the way in which human beings have sought to explain the origins and significance of the world in which they live through stories that demonstrate fundamental similarities over time and place. Elementary themes are shared in the mythologies of very different cultures. Foremost are myths relating to cosmogony, the creation of the universe, the earth and its solar system, theogony, the origin of gods and their genealogy, and etiology, the study of causes and beginnings in general. Certain features also recur: the dualistic principles of good and evil, heaven and earth, light and dark; twins or pairs; the mother figure; and themes of the exploits of heroes, undertaking great challenges or bringing culture to the people. In time these stories act as resources of condensed significance so that merely to name the myth or the mythological character is to unleash a string of associations. Certainly Fabro's practice, with its frequent allusion to classical mythology, owes much to a mythological way of thinking. When making *Guidizio di Paride* in 1979 Fabro introduced a mythological dimension to clarify the work: 'it corresponded to the myth of Paris, something that everyone can understand. This was not an aesthetic attitude on my part; and it induces the viewer to another kind of reflection that goes beyond what is simply visible'.[13] Other works, like *Sisifo (Sisyphus)*, made in 1994 (fig.17), are straightforwardly modern reworkings of ancient myths. 'For me Sisyphus is someone who constitutes an ongoing challenge to fatality, to the gods who condemn him to the eternal task of rolling a large stone uphill. He always succeeds in rolling the stone. There comes a moment when Sisyphus triumphs over the gods, at the top of the hill, and after that it is the gods who triumph. But it is Sisyphus who begins again and finally even the gods are obliged to accept Sisyphus's challenge. Because even if Sisyphus cannot hold the stone at the top of the hill, neither do the gods manage to prevent Sisyphus starting all over again. I find that very contemporary. The question of technique, of work, of all the people who are looking for work and then to think that we are making machines to make work easier'.[14]

Myths are generally a way of committing a truth to memory in a way that makes them universally legible. When Fabro refers to Paris, Demeter or Prometheus, a succession of associations is triggered. In *Penelope* (1972) (fig.16), a work made with needles and green silk thread, 'what interested me initially was a certain kind of manual labour not the myth itself. Penelope represents a woman who wove for ten years'.[15] But Fabro is not only concerned with repackaging mythological truths. He questions the basis of those myths, unravelling the assumptions and experiences on which they are based.

To Giambattista Vico, Neapolitan philosopher of the early eighteenth century, for whom Fabro has declared an enthusiasm, myths (alongside language and rites) were one of the three great doors that lead into the past. Vico propounded a definition of knowledge that had to do not with demonstrable, logical proofs, such as those offered by science, nor with how to do things, nor with the certainties of religious faith, but a knowledge of social and cultural behaviour based on memory and the imagination, which demands that we enter into minds

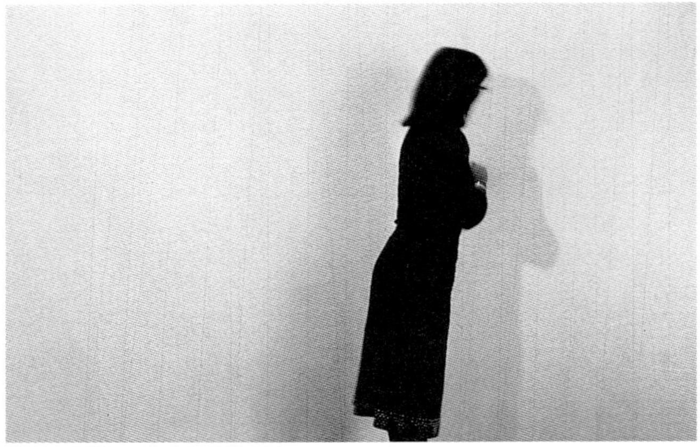

16 Penelope (Penelope), 1972

and situations at some remove from our own. Vico termed this faculty of imaginative insight *fantasia*. Isaiah Berlin characterises Vico's new kind of knowledge as 'like the knowledge we claim of a friend, of his character, of his ways of thought or action, the intuitive sense of the nuances of personality or feeling or ideas'.[16] Anthropomorphic analogy has also been employed by Fabro to describe his art in similar terms: 'There are two possible approaches to the work. An immediate one, as you would approach a person. Someone is likeable or not likeable at all; that is not the whole person but something which brings us closer, which makes us love that person or which compels us to reject him. The second approach comes with better aquaintance, and that obliges us to think each time, to ask questions, not only so as to explain something to us, but perhaps also to provoke, to bring out depth in the relationship. My general poetics would be this: to give the work a personality, something which is similar to a person'.[17]

To Vico, knowledge gained through *fantasia* was superior to other forms of enquiry. To Fabro, art is a form of knowledge, described as *Sophia*, wisdom, and also as thought which unites 'what one shows, what one is, feels, imagines and rationalises'.[18] Other fields of enquiry are now too specialised, too limited in their aims, and thus unable to have the breadth available to art. Again and again, in his writings on art, in his teaching notes and in published interviews Fabro comes back to the central social importance of art. And while much of his work, among its many 'subjects', appears to question the status and function of art, the essence of creation, the 'creative attitude', is, for him, unchanging. Fabro cites Osip Mandelstam, the Russian poet and victim of Stalin, in support of this core definition. Mandelstam, argues Fabro, 'says that the work of the artist is recreation, the protection of creation. And that creation does not change: it may change form but then only to preserve itself. It is like a plant which changes its form biologically according to whether the climate is old or warm, humid or dry, but all those changes are intended to preserve its creative attitude'.[19]

Osip Mandelstam featured in an important work of Fabro's in 1975. *Iconografie (Iconographies)* (fig.18) assembled a group of characters who could never have met in history but who meet in this work at a table prepared in their honour. Osip Mandelstam, Malcolm X, Tantalus, Pier Paolo Pasolini and John the Baptist are amongst those whom Fabro has invoked in the elegant glass bowls that are set out on a long table covered in a carefully pressed white table cloth. In each bowl glass elements float in water. Each fragment is inscribed with the name of one of the five 'martyrs' who have in common only the abuse they suffered for their ideas. As the forms and inscriptions appear to dissolve in the water, images of gatherings round the table contest for place: of summit talks, operating theatres, banquets, of the Last Supper. Fabro's description of how the viewer encounters the work is interesting: 'one must pause at the threshold of significance and look at it from a distance, because that's the way it is, but it is also different, comical and tragic, candy and sweet and horrible. I have never made anything less sublimated or more burdensome in such a frivolous shell'.[20] He asks us to wait and savour the work, to feel its ambivalent impulses, prise open its shell and above all to look at a distance, because to look at a distance is to appreciate all that lies around and outside and beyond the work.

The question of intellectual heritage, and how to protect it, is far more important to Fabro than the issue of originality. Fabro has made a work and an event around the subject of Mandelstam, dedicated to Mandelstam's wife Nadezda who preserved the poet's work by committing his poems to memory and in so doing saved them from the censors and annihilation. Thus Mandelstam's work, a part of his wife's heritage, becomes part of our own intellectual heritage. To Fabro, identity is passed on

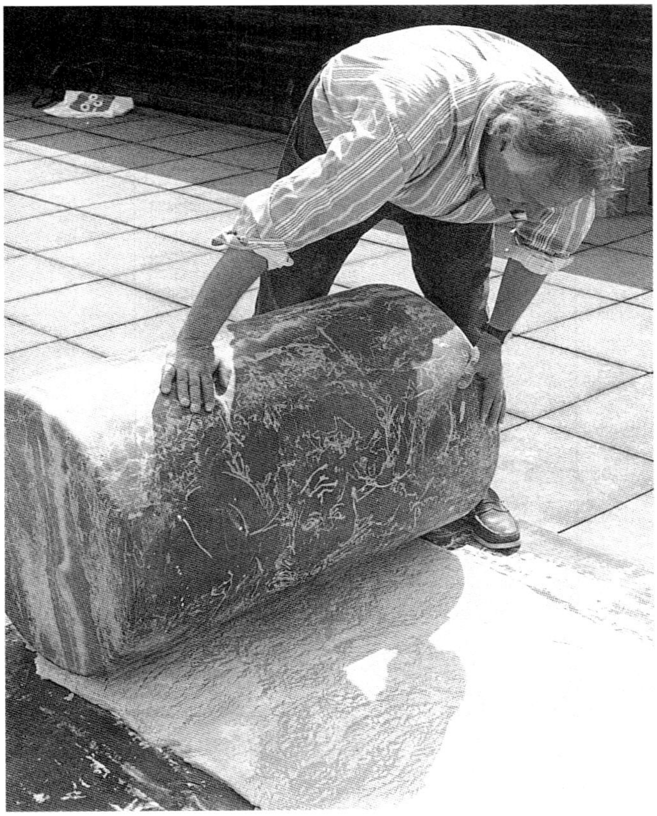

17 Sisifo (Sisyphus), 1994

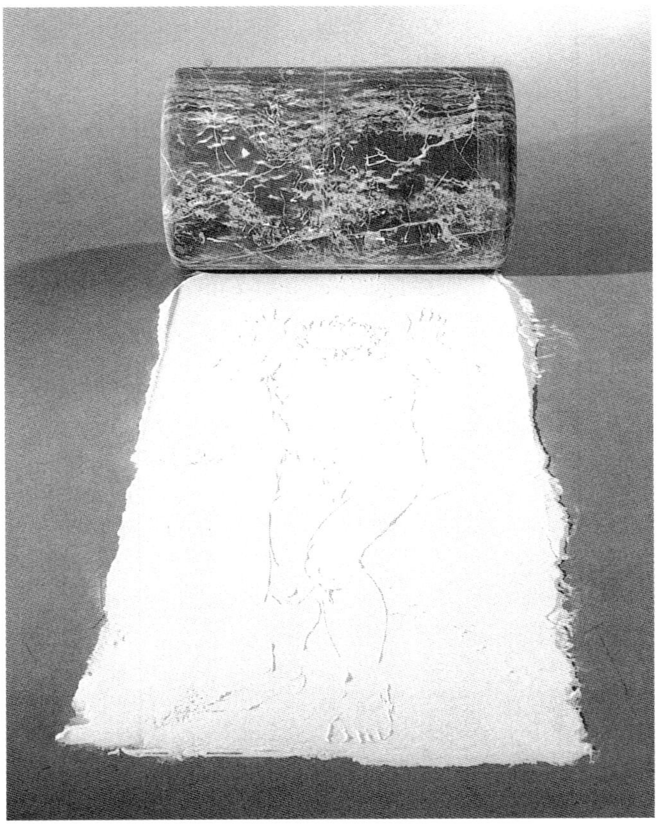

through Nadezda to Mandelstam and on to Dante, with whom Mandelstam identified, and on to Virgil, with whom Dante identified. At the Palais des Beaux-Arts in Brussels in 1990 Fabro mounted an event entitled *Le Caramelle di Nadezda* (fig.20), at which students handed out sweets to visitors. The sweet wrappers were printed with quotations from Nadezda Mandelstam's *Hope against Hope*. The 'event' was intended to recall an episode retold by Nadezda when, during a police raid on their home in 1934, the couple were offered sweets from a tin by one of the Soviet agents. To Fabro *Le Caramelle di Nadezda* was more than a quotation. It was both a way of disseminating her thoughts and also extending Nadezda's memory into cultural memory: 'I told the young people who offered round the sweets that their gesture was a form of availability, being witness to someone who remembers what is in the sweet. Whether they understood it or not was less important. It was like the majority of the Benedictines who did not know what they were copying ... but if we have culture it is largely because of the people who were available to copy the culture, who trusted only in culture'.[21]

Fabro, likewise, is an intellectual who trusts in culture. Chernobyl, Aids, global warming – all have threatened his basic humanism, but Fabro continues to assert a space for art: 'We were in nature, we felt safe there. And suddenly everything in nature became dangerous. Today it is difficult to say where nature begins or ends; we have holes in the atmosphere ... We talk about Chernobyl, but these holes have been developing for much longer, and who knows, Chernobyl is nothing compared to what is happening in biology, Aids ... that is so immense that everything begins to float. Now art is perhaps like a tiny dust particle which remains suspended and on which nature can be recreated. That can become the new meaning of nature'.[22] Acutely aware of the predicament of our times, Fabro is increasingly drawn to themes from the very beginning of time and the early days of Man's probing of his relationship to the universe. Creation mythology lies behind *Prometeo (Prometheus)* made in the aftermath of Chernobyl in 1986 (fig.21). The artist fixed eight pointed stakes on marble columns which formed a circle on the gallery floor. Three of the columns were linked in a triangular diagram by three rulers of the type used in surveying. These rest on the flat tops of the marble bases. Another five rulers were placed to create a pentagon, overlaying and interpenetrating the triangle. There is an indelible and striking contrast between the fragile, inconsequential tools with which we measure the earth and the dense heavy, ancient matter which forms its physical mass. With such simple tools Fabro has made an immensely complex ideogram: static elements (the tools for measuring, for creating certainties) describe a restless spatial zone in which the perception of balance or calm or even of comprehensibility is impossible. When it was first exhibited Fabro commented on the work: 'Prometheus brings into focus a fall. All of our formal concepts derive from a geological concept to which the myth of Prometheus is connected: the relationship between the earth and the gods, conflict and separation. Prometheus is the earth, our capacity to reason: geometry is no more than a rationalisation of the earth'.[23]

Surveyor's instruments, modern ones in the case of *Prometeo*, Roman ones in the case of *Groma* of 1984 (fig.22), are tools associated with observation and the measuring of space. Many of Fabro's works refer to conventional ways of representing space. *Euclide* (1984) and its reformulation as *Paolo Uccello* (1984–5) (fig.23), derive from thinking about the Renaissance discovery of central perspective and the way in which perspective transformed the representation of time. Both works rely on the organising capacity of the human eye and brain as the viewer situates himself in relation to the work: the image, which is virtual, only exists temporarily for the beholder. Central perspective is merely a formal convention developed as a means of comprehending and ordering space. While marvelling

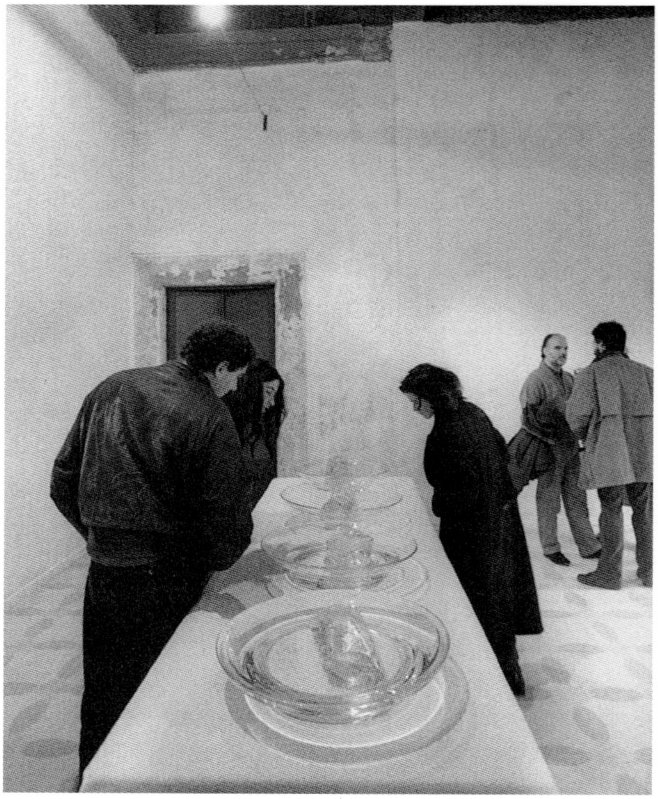

18 Iconografie (Iconographies), 1975

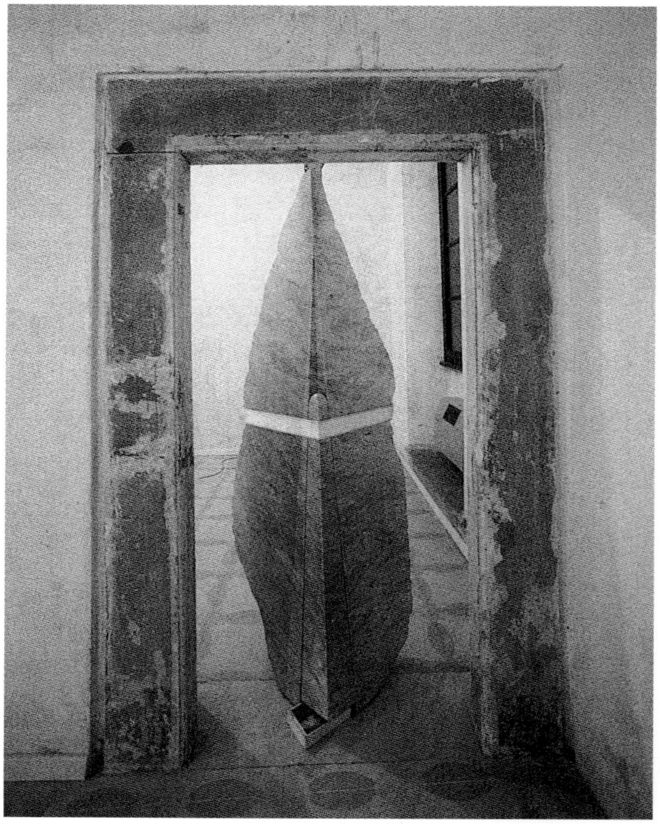

19 Nadezda, 1990

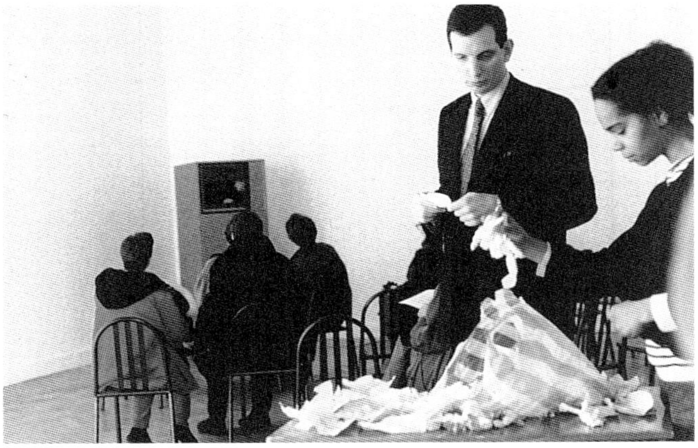

20 Le Caramelle di Nadezda (The Caramels of Nadezda), 1990

at the inventiveness of humanity over time, Fabro nevertheless distrusts conventions and theories. About geometry he recently commented: '[it] exists in all the possible references that can be made with computers today, but it is not reason, it is something which functions for its own sake but does not give us reason'.[24] Hence Fabro's return to Prometheus.

At the time of writing, Fabro's new pieces of work, conceived with the Tate's Duveen Galleries in mind, are still in preparation. Fabro's visits to London and a series of images collaging photographs with drawing, faxed from Milan, have given us some knowledge of his intentions. Working on a scale befitting the space and architectural style of the Sackler Octagon, at the mid-point of the Duveen Galleries, Fabro has once again returned to the theme of geometry. One piece, entitled *La Luna (The Moon)*, is a vertical sculpture, a tapering column around five metres high made from variegated Portorino marble. From a round base the column gradually hollows out as it ascends in such a way that both the profile and the cross-section of the summit follow the shape of a crescent moon. The title of the second piece is *Il Sole (The Sun)*. This sculpture is made from seven pieces of white Carrara marble, which appear to be segments sliced from a column which is tapered and fluted according to the Doric order. The segments are placed at a slight distance one from another, allowing light to penetrate the interior spaces of their forms which have been carved into star-shaped apertures. The star nearest the outside of the piece has nine points; each other in succession has one less point, the 'star' at the opposite end having only three.

Fabro has used the form of the column frequently in his work – as pedestals, or in his *piedi*, and elsewhere, exploring the rich associations of the motif in its own social and iconographic history. The Doric order, with its possible links to an ancient Egyptian prototype, was one of the five 'Orders of Architecture' developed by the Greeks and later the Romans, and systematised by Vitruvius. The orders are both structural and decorative, embracing, at least in their origins, elements of geometry and physics, astrology and alchemy. Fabro has also questioned the Doric order elsewhere, for example in *Esprit de Géométrie, Esprit de Finesse* (fig.24) where the surface fluting is reconciled with the geological structure of the material. In this new work a different and more complex relation is suggested: the column is penetrated by patterns exploring an Islamic model. Islamic design is less concerned with structure, and is more involved with surface pattern than is classical design; the projection of three-dimensional space in a two-dimensional pattern illustrates the Islamic philosophical doctrine of emanation, where manifestation is asserted through dimension: Islamic art is inseparable from Islamic spirituality.[25]

In picturing these spherical elements of the solar system as columns, Fabro recalls an era, long before the birth of Mohammed, when men believed the earth had the form of a cylinder. Speculation about the earth and its relations to the stars and planets has been a fundamental source of human intellectual development, quite apart from its crucial role in the formation of cultural and religious life. Astrology was first explored in the Orient before being inherited by the Greeks, and later adapted and developed in Islamic Arabia before its adoption and Christianisation by the scholastic philosophy of Aquinus. It wasn't until the fifth century BC that some of the concepts crucial to the development of astronomy (inseparable in earlier centuries from astrology) were discovered. Parmenides, the Greek philospher of Nature, first conceived of the earth as a sphere. He also argued that the morning star and the evening star are one and the same and, most importantly, saw the waxing and waning of the moon as an appearance caused by the way in which the partly illuminated sphere of the moon is seen from the earth. Parmenides's great poem opens with an allegorical description

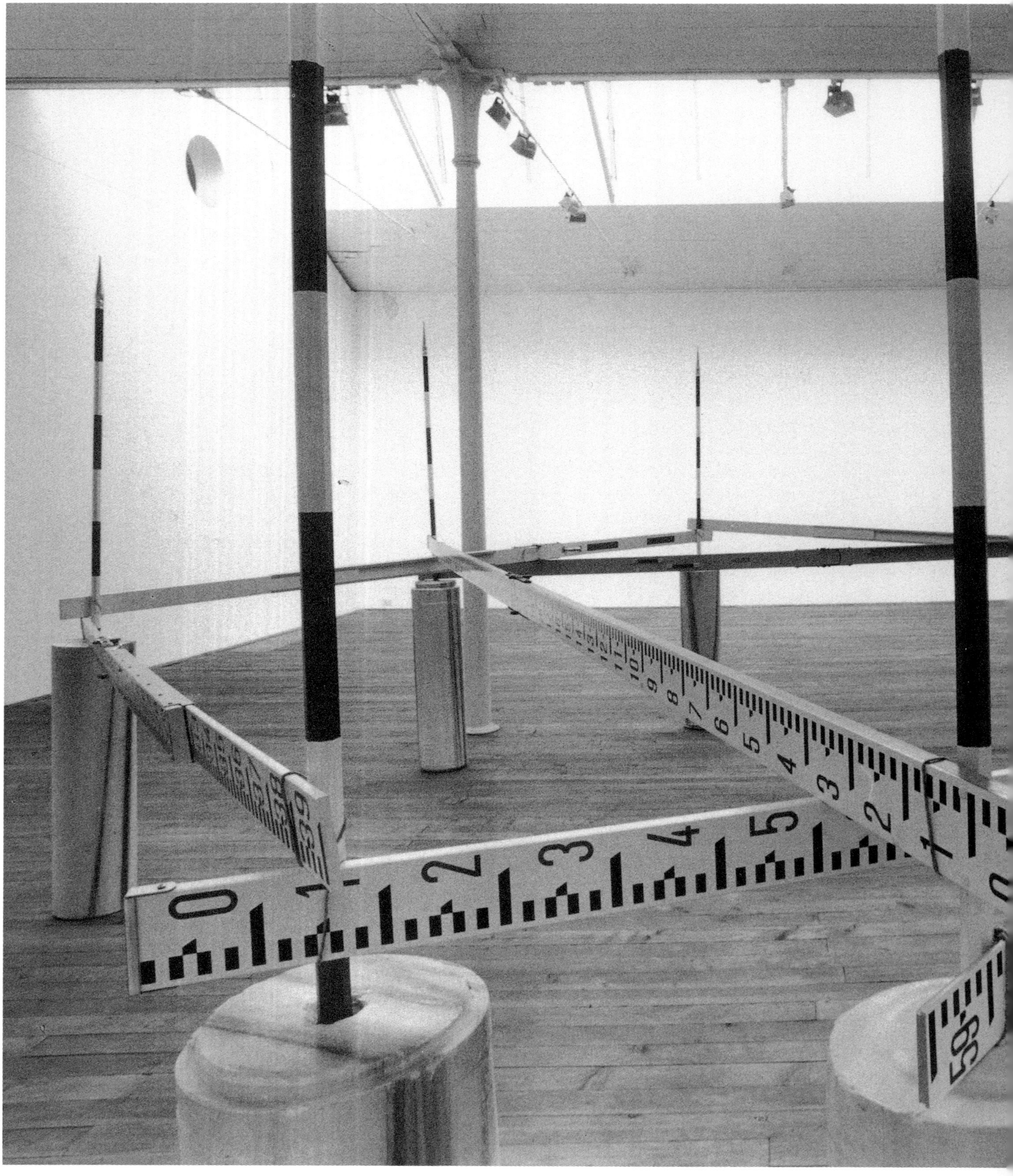

21 Prometeo (Prometheus), 1986

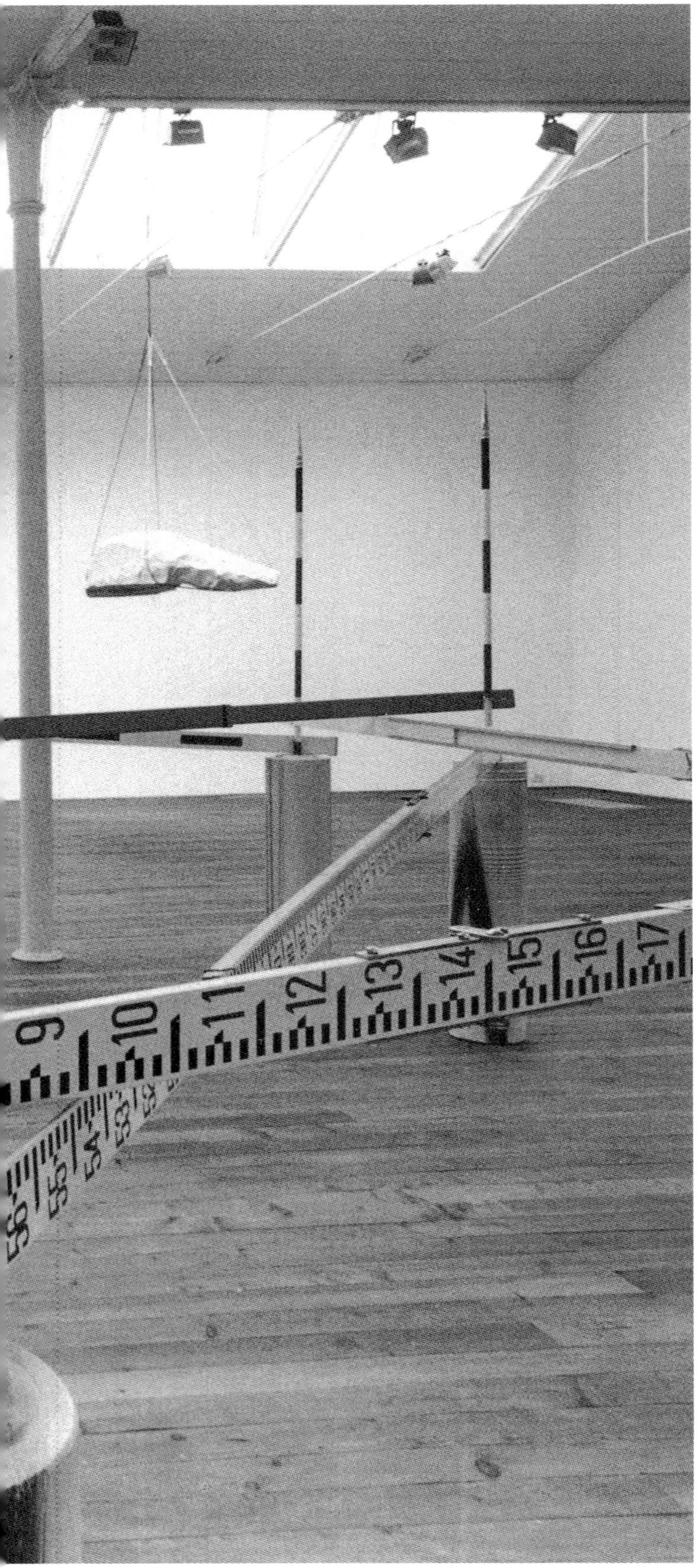

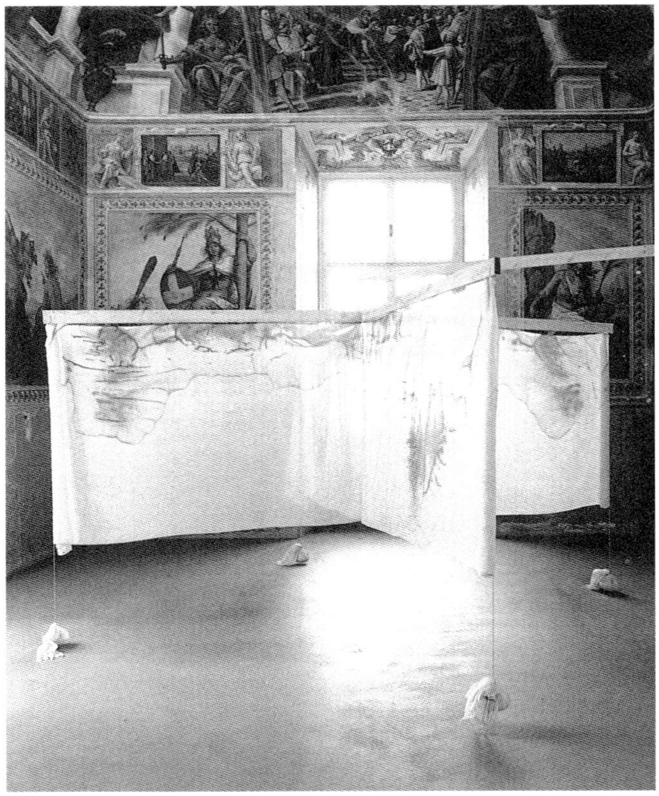

22 Groma, 1984

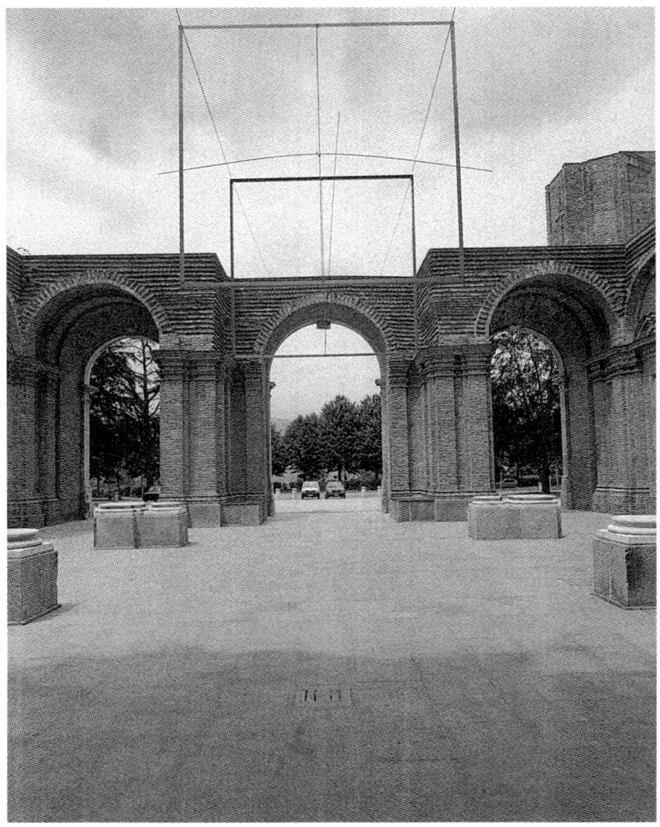

23 Paolo Uccello, 1984–5

24 Esprit de géométrie, esprit de finesse (Spirit of Geometry, Spirit of Finesse), 1984

of his chariot journey through a gate leading from night to day where he is welcomed by a goddess whose revelation provides the remainder of the poem. In an article which Fabro has cited as 'throwing some light' on his work, Karl Popper describes not only Parmenides's astronomical deductions but also his related theory of knowledge with its base in reason and logical proof as opposed to observation.[26] Parmenides deduces the relativity of the sensible world from its ultimate constitution out of two opposite forms, Light and Dark, and the goddess relates the epistemological fall of man to the naming of these elements:

Two forms they made up their minds that they would give names to;
But of these two, one was not permitted to have a name given

Popper, in refutation of most other writers on Parmenides, contests that it was 'light' that could not be named, because the things that light illuminates are, like the moon, intrinsically dark.

Fabro's moon is dark and rooted. His sun is light and mobile, its centre revolving around a complex geometrical scheme. These works, like the table of opposites drawn up by Popper, are rich in contrasts: light and dark, white and black, horizontal and vertical, open and closed, segmented and whole. As so often in Fabro's work, the placing and counter-placing of elements harks back to his very earliest formal experiments with volume, line and space. *La Luna* and *Il Sole* are made up of a number of objects placed in a space, a space in which they are encountered by the viewer, and they create impressions that draw the viewer into a complex chain of references that might lead through time and across cultural boundaries. Through the domed lights of the Octagon the work looks onto a late-twentieth-century sky, not disimiliar to the sky Parmenides must have gazed up at. It is installed in a gallery that was designed and built in the 1930s in a style forged many centuries before. Columns were merely ordered and systematised by Vitruvius. Their roots lie in man's need to shelter himself from the elements, to tie up his vines to face the sun, and to honour the gods in dedicated places of worship.

My last visit to Fabro's studio, six years after the first, was made in order to see a small maquette of *La Luna*, his first thoughts on this project for the Tate Gallery. Aside from this maquette, little had changed in the studio: *Lo Spirato* was still in the corner, still a brooding and disquieting presence. This time I was taken to another working space on the other side of town, the space where Fabro stores and packs his work. The warehouse is approached through the studio of a picture restorer and the accretion of crates and packages and odd materials in Fabro's room was thus framed through visions of landscapes and narratives of oil colour, brushwork and craft in the classical manner. These offered fitting reminders of the heritage that Fabro's career has acknowledged and of his belief that art is not so much about creating new things as about recreating: 'The problem, to progress in art, does not arise; what matters is to preserve it'.[26] Fabro's 'references', whether to historical and mythological figures or to geological and geometrical structures, demonstrate a way in which identity and understanding can be passed on; and he describes the work of art as the 'suitcase' of identity, one which 'like all suitcases, contains patrimonies which date from long ago'.[28]

In Fabro's warehouse and amongst the paraphernalia of his practical affairs was another kind of baggage – equipment designed to facilitate the journeys of a traveller. A car trailer, a tent, a mobile gas burner – all serve as inescapable metaphors for Fabro's intellectual nomadism, his restless energy, his ability to tread lightly but insistently, to set up a temporary home on resistant terrain; an ability to tidy up quickly and move on, leaving behind a meandering trace of impressions belying the singular motivation and sense of responsibility, or vocation, that underpins all his art.

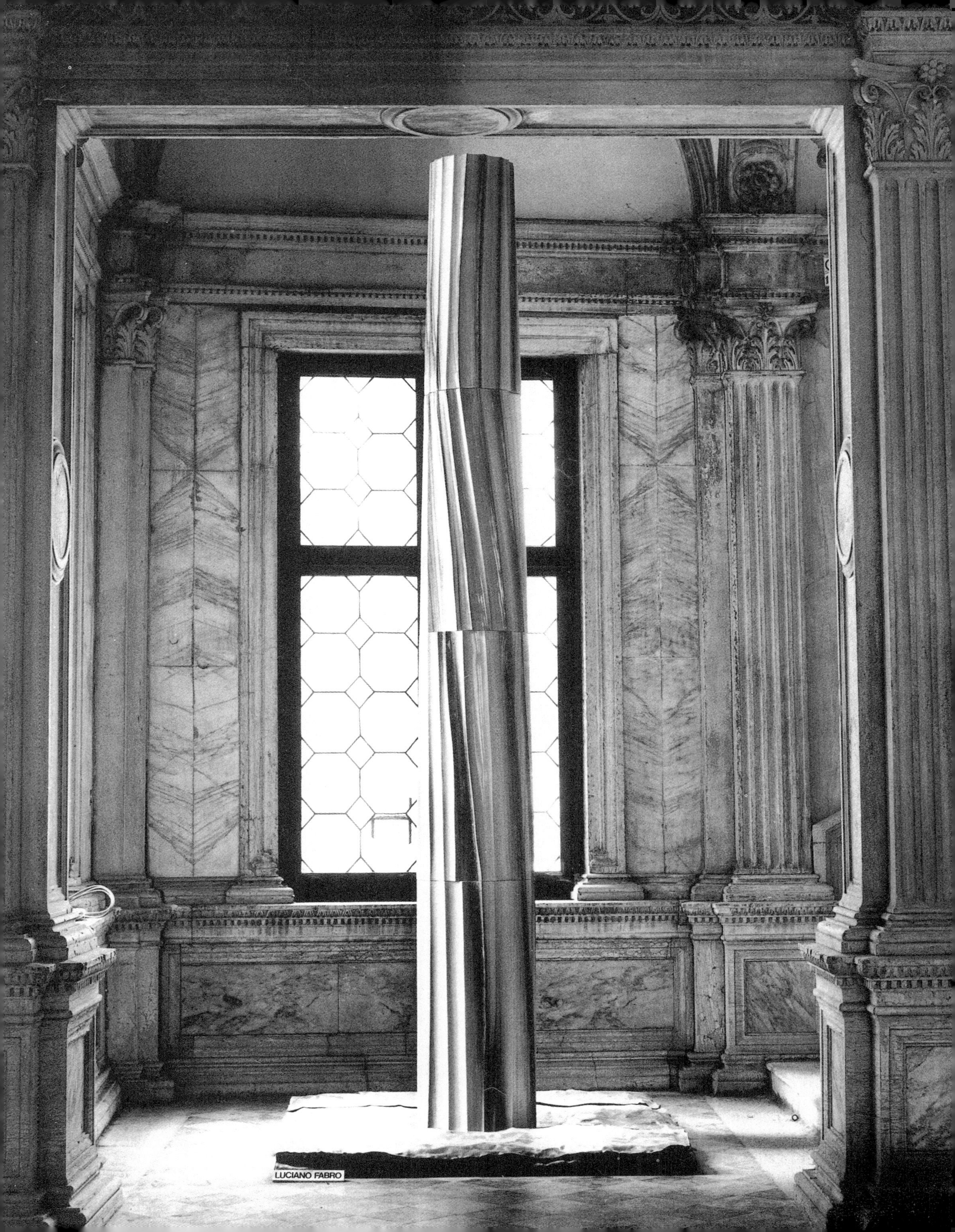

LUCIANO FABRO

Notes

1 Luciano Fabro, 'Vorrei far rilevare', exh. cat., Galleria Vismara, Milan 1965.

2 Luciano Fabro in Carla Lonzi, 'Intervista a Luciano Fabro', *Marcatré*, April 1966, pp.375–9.

3 Luciano Fabro, 'Atti del comune di Milano' (Proceedings of the Milan Municipal Government, 1964) first published in Luciano Fabro, *Attaccapanni*, Turin 1978 and reprinted in *Luciano Fabro*, exh. cat., San Francisco Museum of Modern Art, 1992, pp.25–7.

4 Luciano Fabro, text to accompany exhibition at Galleria Notizie, Turin 1967.

5 Luciano Fabro, *Attaccapanni*, Turin 1978, pp.45–6.

6 Luciano Fabro, 'Vademecum' in *Luciano Fabro*, exh. cat., Museum Boymans-van Beuningen, Rotterdam 1981.

7 Luciano Fabro, ibid.

8 Luciano Fabro, 'Nature', reprinted in *Luciano Fabro*, exh. cat., San Francisco Museum of Modern Art, 1992, p.27.

9 Luciano Fabro, 'Vademecum' in *Luciano Fabro*, exh. cat., Museum Boymans-van Beuningen, Rotterdam 1981.

10 Luciano Fabro quoted by Margit Rowell in 'From James to Bernini, a Pragmatic Sensibility in a Baroque Form', in *Luciano Fabro*, exh. cat., San Francisco Museum of Modern Art, 1992, p.15.

11 Pierluigi Tazzi in *Identité italienne*, exh. cat., Centre Georges Pompidou, Paris 1981, p.487.

12 Luciano Fabro, 'Vademecum' in *Luciano Fabro*, exh. cat., Fundació Joan Miró, Barcelona 1990, p.80.

13 Ibid.

14 Luciano Fabro, interview with Jan Braet in Jan Braet and Luciano Fabro, *'After the rain, a flower opens'*, exh. cat., Open-Air Museum of Sculpture, Middelheim 1994, p.115.

15 Luciano Fabro in *Luciano Fabro*, exh. cat., Fundació Joan Miró, Barcelona 1990.

16 Isaiah Berlin, 'Against the Current', 1979, p.105.

17 Luciano Fabro in Jan Braet and Luciano Fabro, *'After the rain, a flower opens'*, exh. cat., Open-Air Museum of Sculpture, Middelheim 1994, p.26.

18 Ibid., p.27.

19 Ibid., p.68.

20 Luciano Fabro, 'Miracolo a Milano: i punti in comune' in *Data*, Spring 1975.

21 Luciano Fabro in *'After the rain, a flower opens'*, exh. cat., Open-Air Museum of Sculpture, Middelheim 1994, p.65.

22 Ibid., p.37.

23 Luciano Fabro, interview with Francesca Pasini, 'Prometeo irradiato', *Il Manifesto*, October 29, 1986.

24 *'After the rain, a flower opens'*, exh. cat., Open-Air Museum of Sculpture, Middelheim 1994, p.30.

25 Keith Critchlow, *Islamic Patterns: An Analytical and Cosmological Approach*, 1992.

26 Karl Popper, 'How the Moon Might Throw Some of Her Light upon the Two Ways of Parmenides', *Classical Quarterly*, 42, 1992, pp.12–19.

27 *'After the rain, a flower opens'*, exh. cat., Open-Air Museum of Sculpture, Middelheim 1994, p.61.

28 Ibid., p.62.

List of Exhibitions

Luciano was born in Turin in 1936 but brought up in Fruili. In 1959 he moved to Milan where he continues to live and work.

For an extensive biography see the chronology prepared by Jole de Sanna in *Luciano Fabro*, San Francisco Museum of Modern Art, 1992 and continued in *Luciano Fabro*, Portikus, Frankfurt 1995.

Selected Solo Exhibitions

1965 Galleria Vismara, Milan

1967 Galleria Notizie, Turin

1968 *Davanti, dietro, destra, sinistra (Tautologie)*, Galleria Notizie, Turin
O mm (Tautologia), Schultz Restaurant, Solothurn

1969 *Quid nihil nisi minus*, Galleria La Salita, Rome
Galleria de Nieubourg, Milan

1970 *Aktionsraum 1*, Aktionsraum, Munich

1971 Galleria Borgogna, Milan
Galleria Notizie, Turin
Informazione sulla presenza italiana, Incontri Internationali d'Arte, Rome

1973 *Letture parallels 1*, Galleria Borgogna, Milan

1974 *Ogni ordine è contemporaneo d'ogni altro ordine*, Galleria Notizie, Turin
Sinottica degli insiemi e delle proporzioni, Galleria Sperone-Fischer, Rome
Modern Art Agency, Naples
Letture parallels II, Salle Patino, Geneva

1975 *Allestimento teatrale (Cubo di specchi)*, Galleria Bagno Borgonico, Pescara
Iconografie, Galleria Area, Florence

1977 *Attaccapanni*, Galleria Framart, Naples

1979 *Il Giudizio di Paride*, Galleria Mario Pieroni, Rome

1980 *Letture parallele IV*, Padiglione d'Arte Contemporanea, Milan
Habitat delle erbe, Galleria Christian Stein, Turin
Iconografie, Salvatore Ala Gallery, New York

1981 *1962*, Galleria Mario Pieroni, Rome
Sehnsucht, Museum Folkwang, Essen
Duister Kristal: Luciano Fabro, Pier Paolo Pasolini, Museum van Hedendaagse Kunst, Ghent
Museum Boymans-van Beuningen, Rotterdam

1982 *Italia a pennello*, Galleria Banco, Brescia

1983 Neue Galerie Sammlung Ludwig Prize, Aachen
Italia vota, Galleria Massimo Minini, Milan
Pinacoteca Comunale, Loggetta Lombardesca, Ravenna

1984 *Das Deutschland*, Galerie Paul Maenz, Cologne

1986 *Prometeo/Efeso*, Galleria Christian Stein, Milan

1987 *Landscapes*, Fruitmarket Gallery, Edinburgh
Etat, ARC/Musée d'Art Moderne de la Ville de Paris, Paris
Le Nouveau Musée, Villeurbanne
Obélisques, Galerie Sparta-Pelit, Chagny

1988 *Effimero/Ovaie*, Christian Stein Gallery, Turin
Luciano Fabro, con tre nudi che scendono le scale, Galleria Mario Pieroni, Rome
C'est la vie, Palais des Beaux-Arts, Brussels
Basta la vista Eierstöcke, Kunstverein, Munich

1989 *Troubadours*, Galerie Elisabeth Kaufmann, Basel
Castello di Rivoli, Turin
Nord sud est ovest giocano a Shangai, Museo di Capodimonte, Naples
Two Nudes Descending a Staircase Dancing the Boogie-Woogie, Stein Gladstone Gallery, New York

1990 Fundació Joan Miró, Barcelona
Comput di Luciano Fabro e Caramelle di Nadezda Mandelstam, Galleria Christian Stein, Milan

1991 *Ogni ordine è contemporaneo d'ogni altro ordine'*, Museo Casa Bianca, Malo (Vicenza)
Kunstmuseum, Lucerne
Insieme Ensemble Set Menge, Galerie Elisabeth Kaufmann, Basel

1992 *La naissance de Vénus*, Galerie Durand-Dessert, Paris

1994 *Sisifo*, Galerie Micheline Szwajcer, Anvers
Luciano Fabro: Sisyphus, Museum für Gegenwartskunst, Basel
Giardino all'italiana, permanently installed in Picasso-Platz, Basel
Fabroniopera, Palazzo Fabroni, Pistoia

1995 *Luciano Fabro*, Portikus, Frankfurt
Luciano Fabro. Il giorno mi pesa sulla notte, Barbara Gladstone Gallery, New York

1996 *Luciano Fabro: Habiter l'espace*, Musée national d'art moderne, Centre Georges Pompidou, Paris

Selected Group Exhibitions

1967 *Lo Spazio dell'immagine*, Palazzo Trinci, Foligno
Trigon '67. Amblente Environment, Graz, Austria
National Museum of Modern Art, Tokyo
Arte povera, Im spazio, Galleria La Bertesea, Genoa

1968 *Arte povera + azioni povere*, Arsenali dell'Antica Repubblica, Amalfi

1970 *Conceptual Art, Arte povera, Land Art*, Galleria Civica d'Arte Moderna, Turin
Between Man and Matter: Tokyo Biennale '70, Metropolitan Art Gallery, Tokyo
Processi di pensiero visualizzati: lunge italienische Avantgarde, Kunstmuseum, Lucerne

1971 *Arte povera, 13 italienische kunstlers*, Kunstverein, Munich

1972 XXXV Biennale, Venice
Documenta 5, Kassel

1973 *Contemporanea*, Parcheggio di Villa Borghese, Rome

1975 XIII Biennale, Museum of Modern Art, São Paulo, Brazil

1976 *Aptico, il senso della scultura*, Verbania, Pallanza

1980 *Kunst in Europa na '68*, Museum van Hedendaagse Kunst, Citadelpark e Centrum voor Kunst en Cultuur St Pietersplein, Ghent

1981 *Identité italienne. L'art en Italie depuis 1959*, Centre Georges Pompidou, Paris
Westkunst, Museum der Stadt, Cologne

1983 *De Statua*, Stedelijk Van Abbemuseum, Eindhoven

1984 *Il modo italiano*, Institute of Contemporary Art, Los Angeles
Skulptur im 20 Jahrhunderts, Merian Park, Basel
XLI Biennale, Venice
Quartetto (Fabro, Beuys, Nauman, Cucchi), Scuola Grande de San Giovanni Evangelista, Venice
Coerenza in coerenza, Mole Antonelliana, Turin
Alibis, Centre Georges Pompidou, Paris
Idée Progress Ergebniss, Berlin
Ouverture, Museo d'arte contemporanea, Castello di Rivoli,Turin
An International Survey of Recent Painting and Sculpture, The Museum of Modern Art, New York

1985 *Del arte povera a 1985*, Palacio de Cristal and Palacio Velazquez, Madrid
The European Iceberg, Art Gallery of Ontario, Toronto
Nouvelle Biennale de Paris, Paris
Promenades, Pare Lullin, Geneva
The Knot: Arte Povera at P.S.1, The Institute for Art and Urban Resources, New York
Carnegie International, Carnegie Museum of Art, Pittsburgh

1986 *Falls the Shadow: Recent British and European Art*, Hayward Gallery, London
Wien Fluss, Palace of the Secession/Am Steinhof, Vienna
Qu'est-ce que la sculpture moderne?, Centre Georges Pompidou, Paris
XLII Biennale, Venice
Sonsbeeck 86, Arnhem, Netherlands
Chambres d'amis, Museum van Hedendaagse Kunst, Ghent

1987 *Skulptur Projekte 1987*, Milnster
Italie hors d'Italie, Musée des Beaux-Arts, Nîmes
Standing Sculpture, Museo d'arte contemporanea, Castello di Rivoli, Turin

1988 ROSC '88, Dublin
Accademia, Bonnefantenmuseum, Maastricht, Netherlands
Carnegie International, Carnegie Museum of Art, Pittsburgh
Biennale, Sydney

1989 *Bilderstreit*, Ludwig Museum, Cologne
Italian Art in the Twentieth Century, Royal Academy of Arts, London

1990 *Energieen*, Stedelijk Museum, Amsterdam
Casino fantasma, Palazzo Vendramin Calergi, Venice

1991 *Arte povera 1971–Und 20 jahre danach*, Kunstverein München, Munich

1992 *Platzverführung*, Aalen, Stuttgart
Documenta 9, Kassel
Trans-form–Bild Obiekt Skulptur im 20 jahrhundert, Kunstmuseum and Kunsthalle, Basel
Teritorium Artis, Die Kunst-und Ausstellungshalle, Bonn

1993 *Gravity and Grace, The Changing Condition of Sculpture 1965–75*, Hayward Gallery, London

1994 *XLVI Esposizione Internazionale d'Arte, Punti Cardinali dell'Arte*, Venice Biennale

1995 *The Italian Metamorphosis, 1943–1968*, Solomon R. Guggenheim Museum, New York

1996 *Femininmasculin: le sexe de l'art*, Musée national d'art moderne, Centre Georges Pompidou, Paris

Further Reading

The following are the major sources of reference in English

Jan Braet and Luciano Fabro, *'After the rain, a flower opens'*, Open-Air Museum of Sculpture, Middelheim 1994.
John Caldwell, Luciano Fabro, Rudi Fuchs, John Lane and Margit Rowell, *Luciano Fabro*, San Francisco Museum of Art, 1992.
Germano Celant, *Arte Povera*, New York 1969.
Germano Celant, *The Knot: Arte Povera at P.S.1.* 1985.
Luciano Fabro, Mark Francis, *Luciano Fabro: Works 1963–1986*, Fruitmarket Gallery, Edinburgh 1987.
Luciano Fabro, Rudi Fuchs, Johannes Gachnang, John Lane, Werner Oechslin and Daniel Soutif, *Luciano Fabro*, Museo d'arte contemporanea, Castello di Rivoli, Italy 1989.
Luciano Fabro, Catharine Grenier et. al., *Luciano Fabro, Habiter l'espace*, Musée national d'art moderne, Centre Georges Pompidou, Paris 1996–7.
Rudolf Schmitz, 'Such is Art' in *Luciano Fabro*, Portikus, Frankfurt 1995.

Writings by Luciano Fabro

Attaccapanni, Turin 1978
Regole d'arte, Milan 1980
Aufhanger, Cologne 1983
Luciano Fabro: Lavori 1963–1986, Turin 1987
Arte torna arte (lezioni 1987-88), Milan 1989
L'art redevient l'art, Ghent 1990

For a complete list of Fabro's writings and further reading see the extensive bibliography compiled by Silvia Fabro in 'Fabroniopera', Palazzo Fabroni, Pistoia 1994–5.

Photographic Credits

All colour plates: Tate Gallery Photographic Department

Martin Bühler: fig.17 (top)
Giorgio Colombo: fig.23
P. Degobert: fig.17 (bottom)
Luciano Fabro: frontis, figs.1, 3, 6, 7, 8, 15, 16
Silvia Fabro: fig.12
Linda Greeve: fig.20
Nanda Lanfranco: fig.11
Salvatore Licitra: figs.21, 24
A. Maranzano: figs.13, 22
Giovanni Ricci: figs.2, 4, 5, 10, 14, 18, 19
Mussat Sartor: fig.9

List of Illustrated Works

1 *Lo Spirato (The Deceased)*, 1968–73
Marble
190 x 90 cm
Collectively owned, care of the artist

2 *Buco (Hole)*, 1963
Glass, silver and lacquer, iron base
Rectangular glass 110 x 80 cm; circular glass 70 x 70 cm
Collection of the artist

3 *Ruota (Wheel)*, 1964
Stainless steel
142 x 51 x 1 cm
Private collection

4 *Tondo e rettangolo (Circle and Rectangle)*, 1964
Glass, silver and lacquer, iron base
120 x 80 cm
Collection of the artist

5 *Foro Ø 8mm – Tautologia*
(8mm Ø Perforation – Tautology), 1967
Stainless steel
198.1 x 99.7 cm
Private collection

6 *Pavimento – Tautologia (Floor – Tautology)*, 1967
Floor and newspaper
Dimensions variable

7 *Italia del dolore (Italy of Pain)*, 1975
Road map of Italy, de ruta cloth, iron and string
150 x 80 cm
Private collection

8 *Italia d'oro (Golden Italy)*, 1971
Bronze and steel
75 x 45 cm
Collection of the artist

9 *Italia feticcio (Fetish Italy)*, 1981
Copper
160 x 65 x 40 cm

10 *Piedi (Feet)*, 1968–71
Shantung silk, metal and marble
Dimensions variable
Various collections

11 *La nascita di Venere (The Birth of Venus)*, 1992
Onyx, marble
263 x 70 x 118 cm
Collection Bonnefantenmuseum, Maastricht

12 *Kronus*, 1991
Marble
250 x 200 x 170 cm
Private collection

13 *Due nudi che scendono le scale ballando il Boogie-Woogie*
(Two Nudes Descending a Staircase Dancing the Boogie-Woogie), 1989
Iron, marble, nylon, oil and casette recorder
Dimensions variable
Collection Art Gallery of Ontario, Toronto

14 *Ovaie (Ovaries)*, 1988
Marble and steel
2 elements, overall 7.5 x 1125 x 150 cm
Tate Gallery, London
[3 versions]

15 *Il Giudizio di Paride (The Judgement of Paris)*, 1979
Terracotta
4 elements 55 x 45, 52 x 45, 49 x 45, 71 x 55 cm
Collection Stedelijk Van Abbemuseum, Endhoven

16 *Penelope (Penelope)*, 1972
Wall, needles and silk thread
Dimensions variable

17 *Sisifo (Sisyphus)*, 1994
Portorino marble, flour
100 x 60 x 200 cm
[5 versions]

18 *Iconografie (Iconographies)*, 1975
Glass, distilled water, table and cloth
800 x 100 x 80 cm
[2 versions; *Private collection; Collection Museum Van Hedendaags Kunst, Gand*]

19 *Nadezda*, 1990
Bardiglio marble, strap, copy of *Hope against Hope* by Nadezda Mandelstam
published in the language of the country in which the work is exhibited
237 x 216 cm
Collection of the artist

20 *Le Caramelle di Nadezda (The Caramels of Nadezda)*, 1990
Event staged at the Palais des Beaux-Arts, Brussels

21 *Prometeo (Prometheus)*, 1986
Zebrino marble, measuring rods and poles, cord
Overall 1986 x 250 cm

22 *Groma*, 1984
Cloth, wood and sand
Dimensions variable
Collection of the artist

23 *Paolo Uccello*, 1984–5
Iron and steel
400 x 400 x 400 cm
Collection of the artist

24 *Esprit de géométrie, esprit de finesse*
(Spirit of Geometry, Spirit of Finesse), 1984
Zebrino marble, lead
400 x 50 x 50 cm
Collection of the artist

I would like to leave a message

Art is that attitude within natural phenomena, be it physical or spiritual, which modifies the process, augmenting its definition: after the artistic act the phenomenon can no longer be defined as before.

All of our senses are set in motion; our entire body reacts when we are interested in something, when we come into contact with something or someone. There is no great difference between two things and two people which come into contact. When the wind meets leaves, it makes them react at a deep level and not only on the surface, to the point when, with time, they will better adapt to the wind, at the moment and at the time when the wind changes its course, its heat, its smell. Thus everything interacts with everything else and this interaction tends toward the harmonisation of things among themselves, or rather, towards the placement of one thing next to another so that the result is art. This disposition within natural phenomena includes adaptation, defines selection, establishes new processes. If cacti have thorns and are barrels of water, it is due to an act of some individual cactus, in some moment, which permitted it to survive and at the same time to create its aesthetic, that is, to become in harmony with the context. At the moment in which it harmonised, it defined its function: it will be visual, olfactory, gustatory, spatial, sensitive and intellectual nutrition of the context. These acts become related to other acts, and together they create an aesthetic. This aesthetic will permit a definition of a series of phenomena and functions.

These acts give us the elements of difference and harmony. I mean that only through a harmonic comparison can we differentiate; I also mean that the elements, by interacting, left chaos and ended the cosmos.

The harmonic interaction determines the pleasure, order, and action. Action includes more and more varied elements and creates harmony in continuous modification. The motor of this action is harmony itself.

I call this process of locomotive harmony the artistic act. The artistic act would be the spark which precedes the moment of the realisation of phenomena, changes, discoveries, inventions, and the birth of systems. Even if I do not know how a bird or a stone reflected on this, I think that some form of reflection is common among all elements.

I call this common reflection 'aesthetic reflection', and it is that which moves me when I see a sunset or the pattern of a butterfly, but also it is my own capacity to metabolise a fruit both by eating it and by drawing it, by formulating a geometry through it.

We generally pay more attention to the moments following the artistic act because they seem more concrete to us. But, I repeat, at this point everything has already happened, and we are not able to do anything but evaluate the consequences, in one field or another, in what is more convenient for us at that moment. It is for this reason that for the scientist the artistic act becomes scientific, for the religious man it becomes religious, for the person who puts all his energy into daily things it becomes quotidian.

By this I do not mean that everyone is busy doing artistic acts in equal measure. I am only saying that the artistic act is natural and is distributed naturally. I also would like to repeat that, since it is the origin of other acts, it precedes them and distinguishes among them. And thus I have arrived at my point, which I think is clear enough to say that the artistic act distinguishes itself from the work of art as such. Hence, to make works of art does not mean in itself to live artistic acts, but rather to undertake the responsibility of transmitting the artistic act frequently. The artist is the person who realises the artistic act in an image, in that which the masters of art – the Greeks – called 'Idea'.

I can testify that the Idea manifests itself as an image. I can testify that the mark of the artist consists of two basic elements: one is that the image presents itself to him absolutely clearly and distinctly, the other is that he must have the obsession to give consistency to this image.

Now let's try to give a time to the work of art. I place this time at the moment in which the artist has the revelation of things, he sees things as if for the first time, as if it were the day of creation; he sees them with enthusiasm, as when we discover a splendid view. He sees things emerge brilliantly from the chaos that is customs and prejudices, from the ruins of what was harmonious beforehand.

What does the artist do? Having determined a creative moment, he abstracts it from its context, and from its natural consequences. Like the scientist, he determines a law out of a series of phenomenon. Thus the artist determines the artistic act that is the origin of a phenomena. In order to isolate it to give it form, in order to highlight it, he transfers it onto some sort of screen or support. Just as the light of bodies is fixed onto the cinematographic film, once in a while the artistic act is fixed with words, sound, material, space, and thousands of other ways which are more or less familiar to us. Those which are more familiar to us are the ones we call music, poetry, painting, architecture, sculpture. These are nothing but screens, supports whose adherence to the artistic act must be checked on and modified from time to time. I repeat that the artistic act in itself is not identifiable in nature by its effects, nor by its determination of the development of the natural bodies and it is not comparable except in the consequences which it determines upon the natural bodies.

When artistic act and support adhere we have the work of art, or the artistic act takes on a body of its own. The work of art gives us the artistic act isolated from the consequences on the natural bodies. One of the ways to define this difference is to use very basic supports in the work of art, such as stone in sculpture, coloured mixtures in painting, and also to use very rudimentary techniques. Think of the technology of the artistic act which corresponds in nature to the colours of a flower, and compare it with that which was used in a work of art by Matisse in order to paint the same flower: in the case of nature, the artistic act has arranged all the possible and imaginable elements of our imagination and intelligence. In the case of the work of art by Matisse, it was more a matter of arranging the coloured pigments onto a piece of canvas.

But here is where the miracle occurs: if that arrangement of spots of colours had fallen on your shoes you'd have to throw them away, but if you organise them on that poor support they must yield the same artistic act which contributed to the birth of that flower. But one would think that the relation of the two artistic acts is a formal one, since there is a resemblance between the two flowers, the one in nature and the one painted by Matisse. But instead, the resemblance is only passing; I could say that what makes the work of art and the images in nature resemble one another is a pentagram which artists adopt in order to better make the artistic acts of the work of art in tune with the artistic acts of the work of nature.

From this discussion, one would think that all the effectiveness lies in the artistic act, in the work of art. In the economy of the species, then, one cannot understand why some people insisted on constructing coloured surfaces from the beginning of humanity, by engraving stones and collecting them, on organising sounds, words, images, sensations. Since the beginning, man has reflected both on death by disharmony, as well as on death by regression. Some dedicated themselves to combat regression by knowledge, and that is how religious, civil and natural knowledge came about. Others, in order to combat death by disharmony, dedicated themselves to that which I call the artistic act. These people called themselves artists.

Elements which die lose the complex experience acquired in the vital processes. An abandoned field, or one in which growth is destroyed, is transformed into a desert, and as a dead zone it becomes a danger of death for other beings.

This artistic act is common, then, to all beings and also to man; about man we even know something further; we know that he senses when the order of things is in a state of crisis, when aesthetics, or the order of things, are going into a state of crisis. When I say that the aesthetics of things can go into a state of crisis, I include also the aesthetics of thought, the aesthetics of conscience: I mean any kind of harmonious activity. The understanding of an artistic act is not arbitrary but rather it answers the state of necessity. It happens only when it is necessary. If, however, it didn't happen when it was necessary, we would have the end of that being.

I believe that when artistic acts happen we should be happy. But once one understands that the manifestation of a phenomenon is a question of art, a sense of responsibility arises which doesn't make one very happy.

In practice, when things are dying, they wither, they protract beyond their size; this depends on the fact that the necessary artistic facts do not happen. If one does not listen to music, one loses one's ear for music; if one does not pay attention to plants, they all end up in the same state; if one is not careful to treat people with interest, or better, with love, they become unbearable. In each of these cases we have death by disharmony. I think of man's terror when he discovered this, and I think that he was obligated to find a solution by writing his memories of the artistic acts and the works of art in the form of a diary. These works are a memory of harmonious solutions, harmonies by which the ear can remain exercised, the eye attentive, and the feelings awake. This is an intelligence ready for the continual future of artistic acts, so that our senses remain in motion in a way that they can adequately interact with everything and this interaction can tend toward the harmonisation of things among themselves, to the placement of one thing next to another so that the result is art.

Luciano Fabro
San Francisco, 30 September 1992

The sun and the moon

The sun like a cluster of rays, just like the fluting of the column, around a nucleus of geometric emptiness and full of stars. The moon is constructed so as to reconcile the flow with the beating of time; I do not think anyone will be offended that it is influenced by Piranesi and Brancusi.

These works are born of a kind of observation of the relationship between the cosmos and the image, or between order and image. What intrigues me is that the image of the cosmos is formless at first and gains form only through knowledge.

I have often called the state of mind of this everyday sensation 'Day weighs on my night'.

Luciano Fabro
January 1997

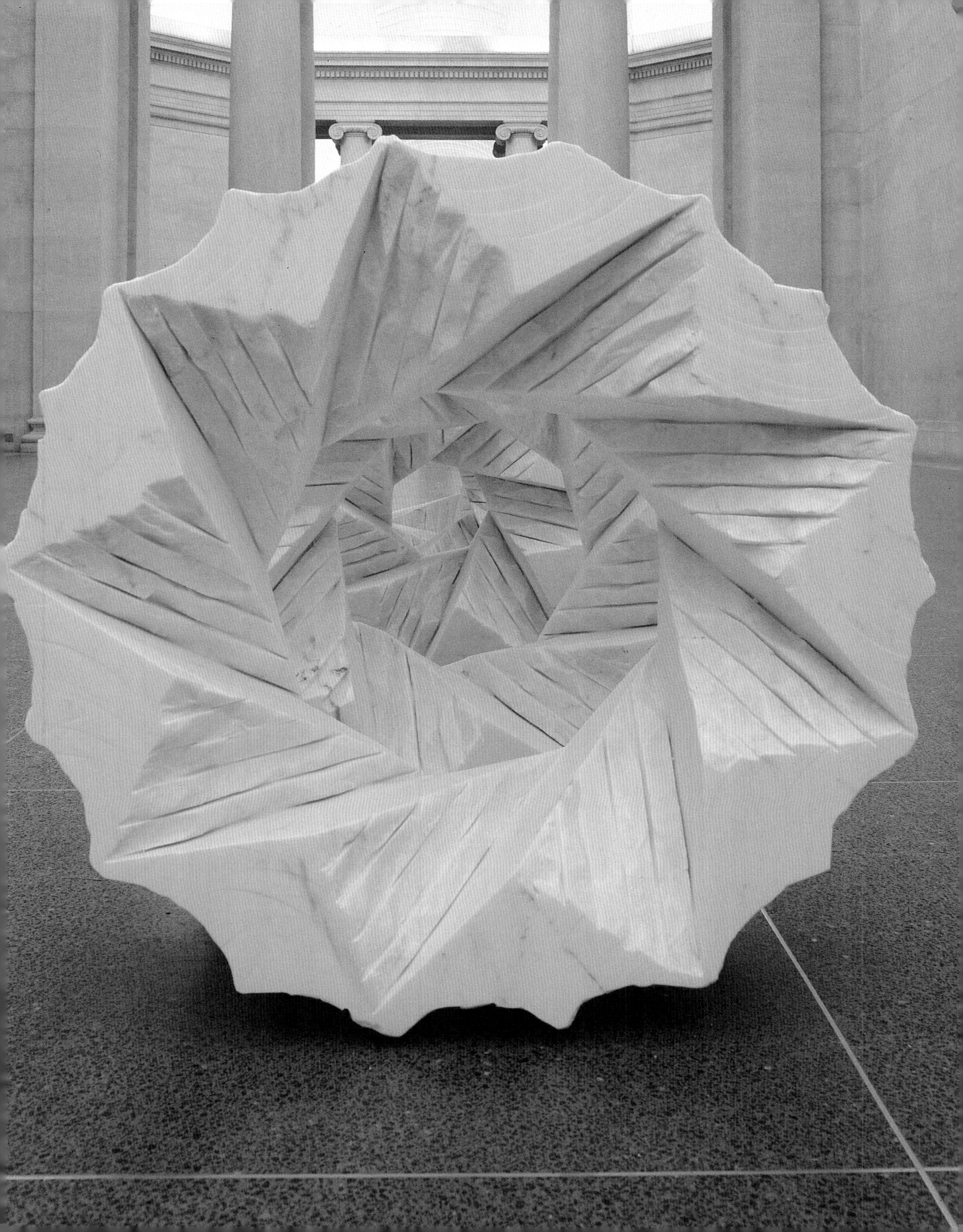

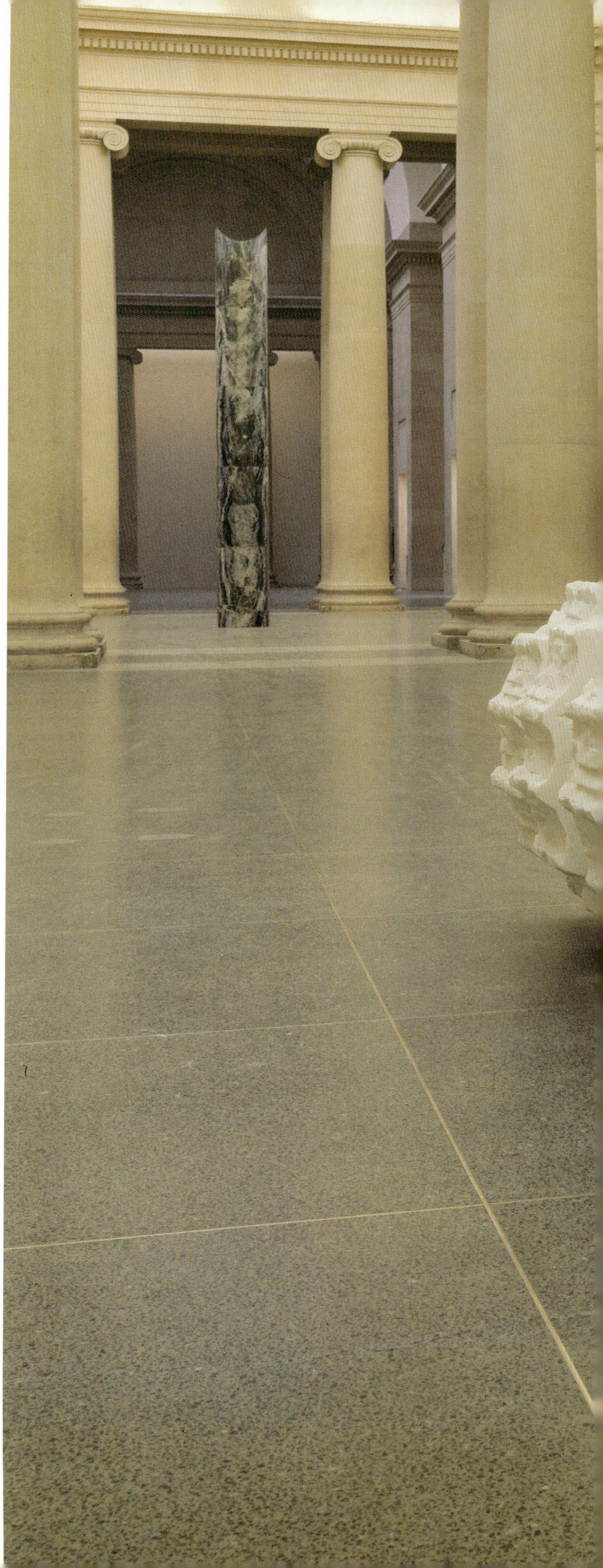

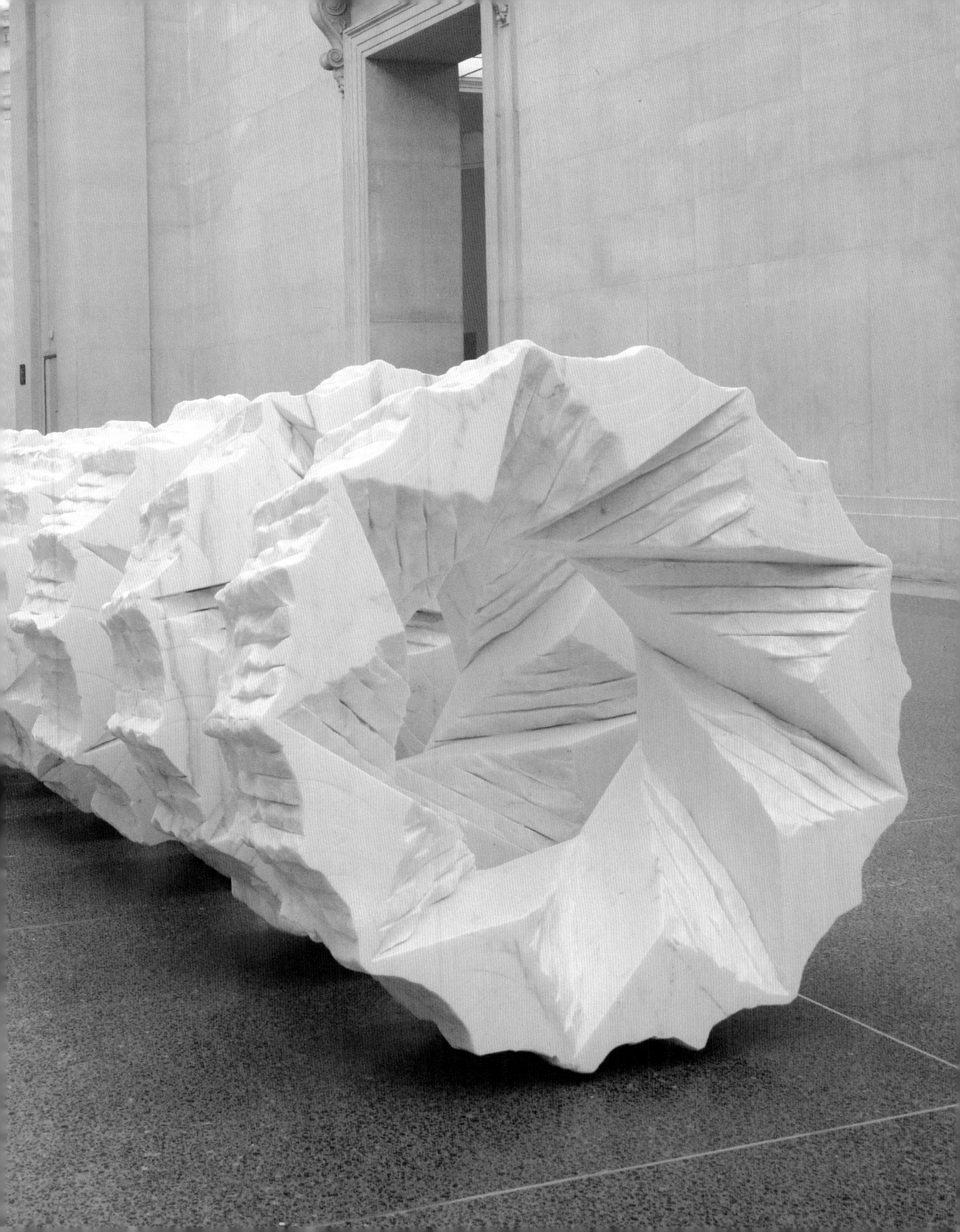

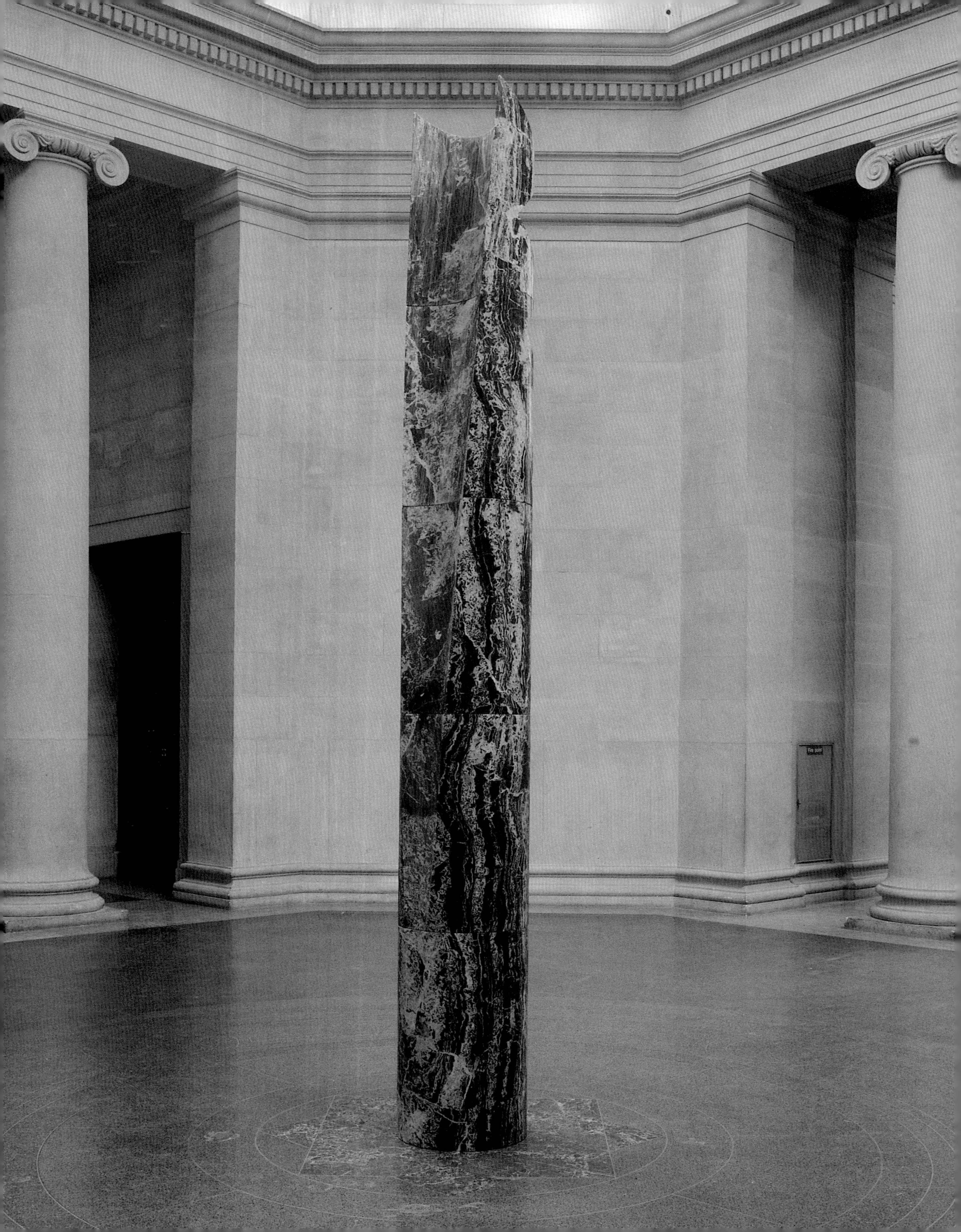

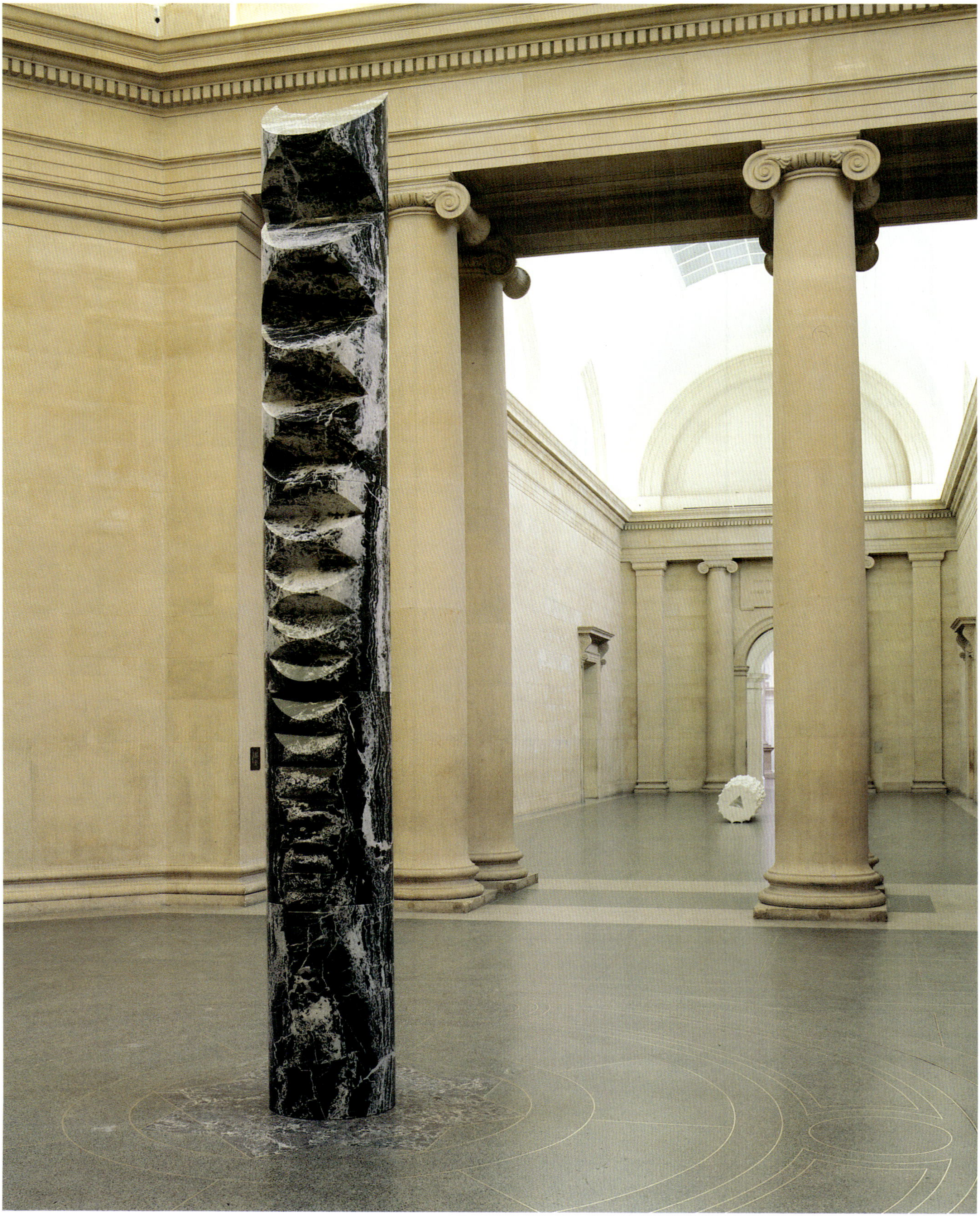
La Luna (The Moon), 1997

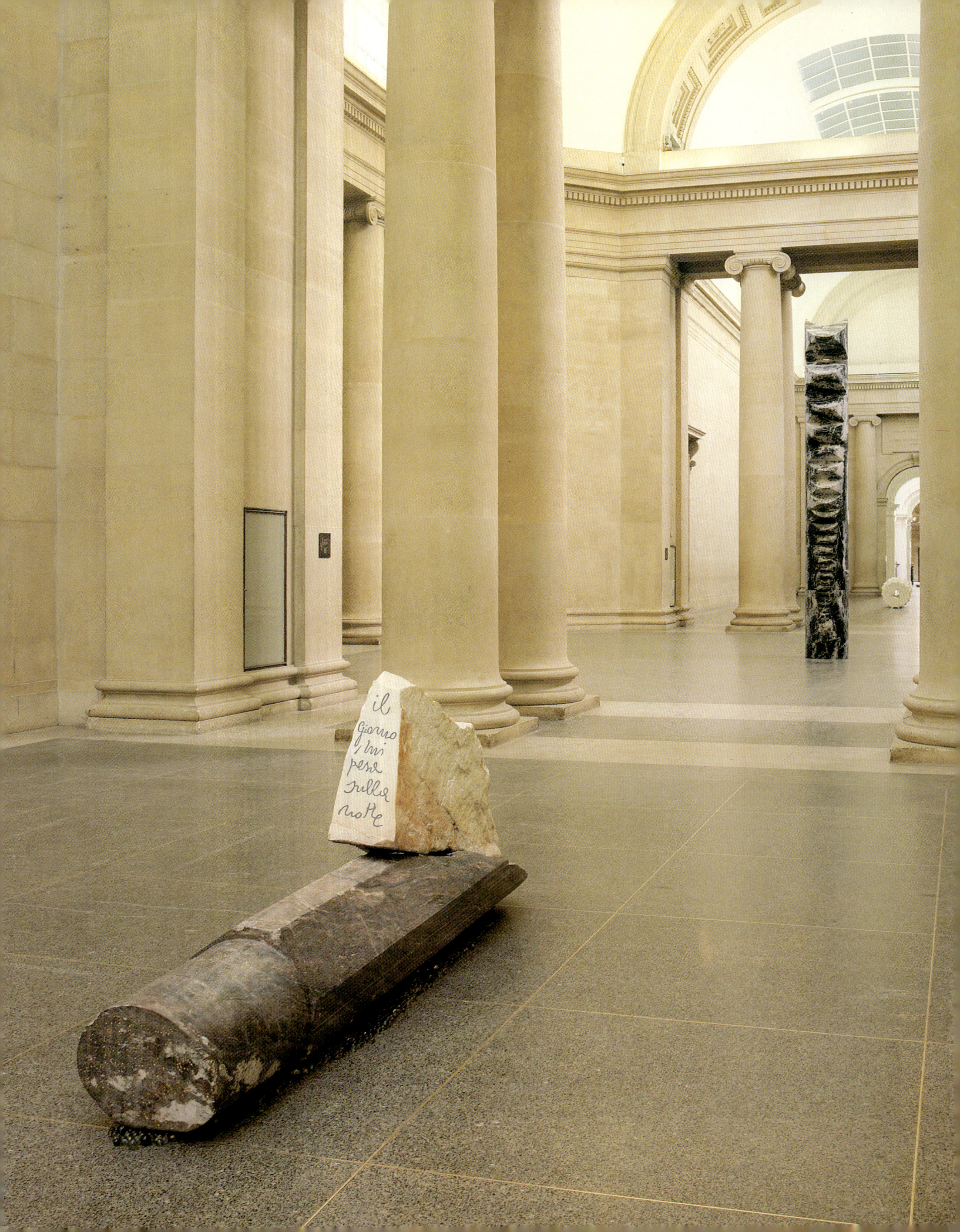
il
giorno
pesa
sulla
notte

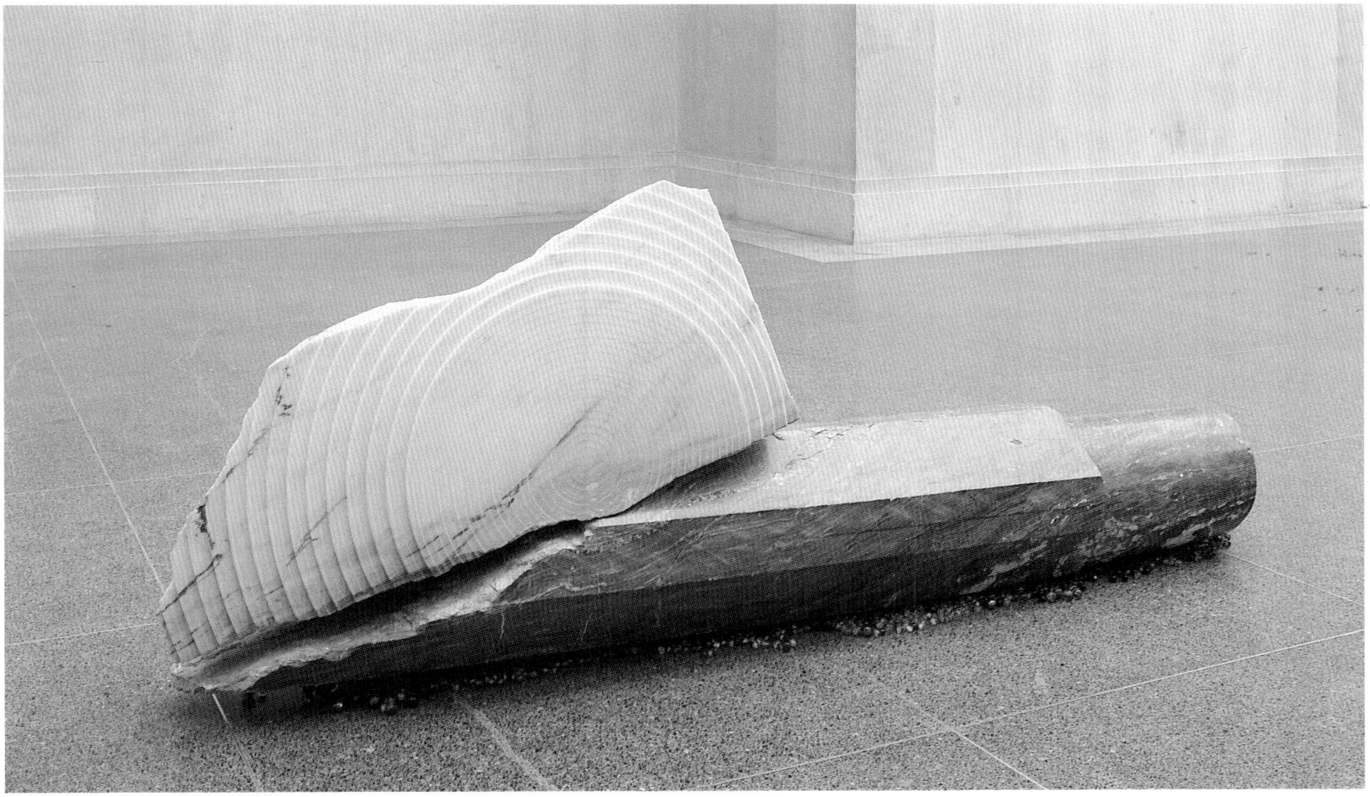

Above and left Il Giorno Mi Pesa Sulla Notte 1 (Day Weighs on My Night 1), 1994

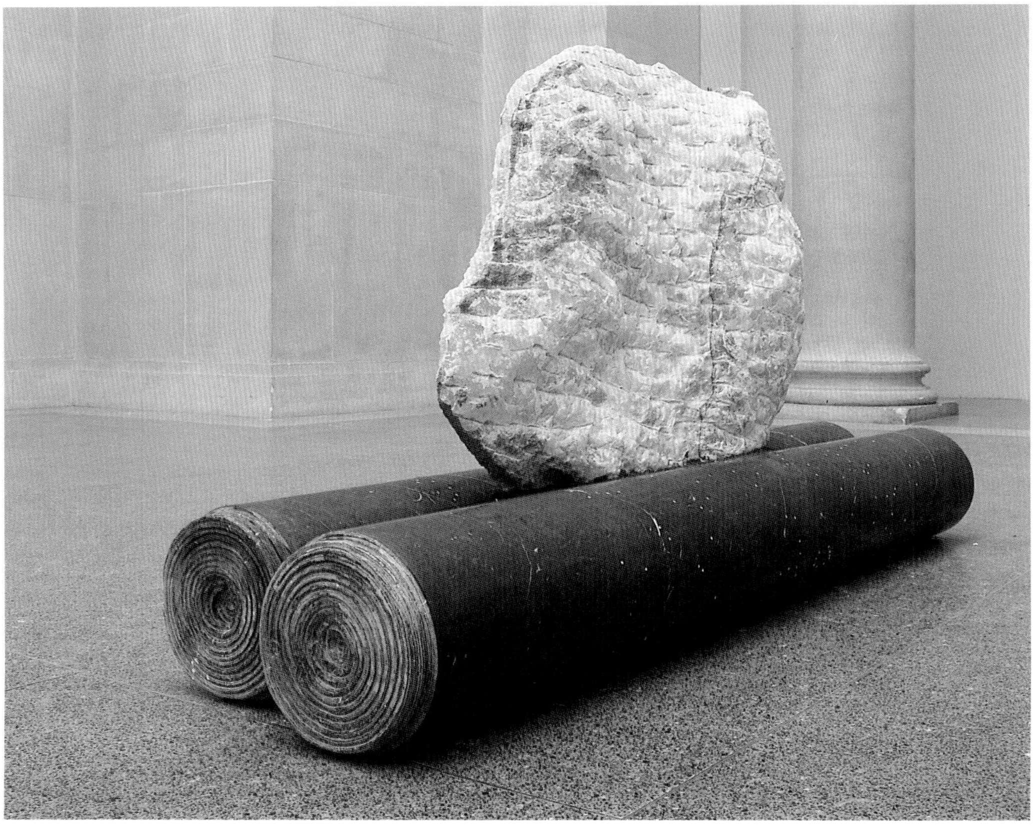

Il Giorno Mi Pesa Sulla Notte 2 (Day Weighs on My Night 2), 1996

List of Exhibited Works

Colour photography by Marcus Leith of the Tate Gallery
Photographic Department

Il Sole (The Sun), 1997
Carrara marble
Seven sections, overall dimensions 91.5 x 93 x 313 cm
Collection of the Artist
Pages 37, 38–9

La Luna (The Moon), 1997
Portorino marble
Five sections, overall dimensions 485 x 56 cm (diam. at base)
Collection of the Artist
Pages 40, 41

Il Giorno Mi Pesa Sulla Notte 1 (Day Weighs on My Night 1), 1994
Marble, marbles, gold and lead
100.3 x 38 x 256.5 cm
Collection of the Artist
Pages 42, 43

Il Giorno Mi Pesa Sulla Notte 2 (Day Weighs on My Night 2), 1996
Marble and earth
135 x 68 x 255 cm
Collection of the Artist
Page 43